P9-BJE-092

$\mathcal{T}$o

_____

$\mathcal{F}$ROM

_____

$\mathcal{M}$ESSAGE

_____

_____

_____

_____

Promises from God for When You Doubt

© 2003 Christian Art Gifts, RSA
Christian Art Gifts, Lombard, IL

Compiled by Wilma Le Roux and Lynette Douglas
Designed by Christian Art Gifts

ISBN 1-86920-072-1

Printed in China

03 04 05 06 07 08 09 10 11 12 – 10 9 8 7 6 5 4 3 2 1

PROMISES
FROM GOD FOR
WHEN
YOU DOUBT

christian
art gifts

CONTENTS

$\mathcal{I}$NTRODUCTION

Let us hold unswervingly to the hope we profess,
for he who promised is faithful.

Hebrews 10:23, NIV

Faithfulness is one of the most treasured values in life. And yet so often we are disappointed by promises that have been broken – both those we make and those that are made to us. It is therefore no wonder that our soul responds with gratitude to the unfailing faithfulness of God.

Life is full of daily trials and tribulations that cause despair and hopelessness, and sometimes we even begin to wonder if God truly hears our cries. But He is faithful to all His promises, and His Word encourages us to hold fast to His promises in times of doubt, in loneliness, in discouragement, and in adversity. Let the promises of God soak into your heart and let the hope of His goodness renew your faith in His love for you.

ANXIETY

"Let not your heart be troubled: ye believe in God, believe also in me."

John 14:1, KJV

Corrie ten Boom said: "Worrying does not empty tomorrow of its grief; it only deprives today of its power." There are few things in life more destructive than worry. Worry deprives you of your physical and intellectual abilites. It causes so much tension that you are often reduced to a state of helplessness and despair. The vitality drains from your life and actions.

If we want to experience peace of mind in this fast-paced world with all its temptations and trials, we should follow the example of Jesus. His life was completely and unconditionally surrendered to the care of His heavenly Father. You, too, should place your life with its burdens, problems and worries entirely in God's hands. Then you will be able to face life with strength and peace of mind.

GOD'S PROMISES

FOR THE ANXIOUS

Humble yourselves, therefore, under God's mighty hand, that he may lift you up in due time. Cast all your anxiety on him because he cares for you.

1 Peter 5:6-7, NIV

Unto him that is able to do exceeding abundantly above all that we ask or think, according to the power that worketh in us, Unto him be glory in the church by Christ Jesus throughout all ages, world without end.

Ephesians 3:20-21, KJV

Search me, O God, and know my heart; try me, and know my anxieties; and see if there is any wicked way in me, and lead me in the way everlasting.

Psalm 139:23-24, NKJV

"And which of you by being anxious can add a single hour to his span of life? If then you are not able to do as small a thing as that, why are you anxious about the rest?"

Luke 12:25-26, ESV

I will say of the LORD, He is my refuge and my fortress: my God; in him will I trust.

Psalm 91:2, KJV

"Come to me, all who labor and are heavy laden, and I will give you rest. Take my yoke upon you, and learn from me, for I am gentle and lowly in heart, and you will find rest for your souls."

Matthew 11:28-29, ESV

"Therefore I tell you, do not worry about your life, what you will eat or drink; or about your body, what you will wear. Is not life more important than food, and the body more important than clothes? Look at the birds of the air; they do not sow or reap or store away in barns, and yet your heavenly Father feeds them. Are you not much more valuable than they? Who of you by worrying can add a single hour to his life?"

Matthew 6:25-27, NIV

Be anxious for nothing, but in everything by prayer and supplication, with thanksgiving, let your requests be made known to God; and the peace of God, which surpasses all understanding, will guard your hearts and minds through Christ Jesus.

Philippians 4:6-7, NKJV

Anxiety in a man's heart weighs him down,
but a good word makes him glad.

Proverbs 12:25, ESV

The eyes of the Lord are on the righteous,
and His ears are open to their prayers.

1 Peter 3:12, NKJV

Say to those who have an anxious heart,
"Be strong; fear not! Behold, your God will
come with vengeance, with the recompense
of God. He will come and save you."

Isaiah 35:4, ESV

I lay down and slept; I awoke, for the LORD
sustained me.

Psalm 3:5, NKJV

Cast your burden on the LORD, and He
shall sustain you; He shall never permit
the righteous to be moved.

Psalm 55:22, NKJV

Commit thy way unto the LORD; trust also
in him; and he shall bring it to pass.

Psalm 37:5, KJV

CHOSEN

*"For you are a people holy to the LORD your God.
The LORD your God has chosen you to be a people
for his treasured possession."*

Deuteronomy 7:6 ESV

There are many people who express their
dissatisfaction with their destiny. Some feel
that life is unfair. Regardless of the reason,
these people are inclined to adopt a negative
and defeatist attitude towards life and, as a
result, they withdraw and become lonely
people.

If things are not turning out right for
you at this moment, remember that you
are a child of God and that He loves you
dearly. God, in His mercy, chose you to be
His friend and He offers you the life-giving
strength of the Holy Spirit to enable you
to live life to the full. Do not succumb to
negative experiences and influences but,
through Jesus Christ, rise above them and
live your life the way He intended it to be.
Remember what Jesus said, *"... I have come
that they may have life, and have it to the
full"* (Jn. 10:10, NIV).

The Lord's

CHOSEN

But you are a chosen people, a royal priesthood, a holy nation, a people belonging to God, that you may declare the praises of him who called you out of darkness into his wonderful light.

1 Peter 2:9, NIV

"If ye were of the world, the world would love his own: but because ye are not of the world, but I have chosen you out of the world, therefore the world hateth you. Remember the word that I said unto you, The servant is not greater than his lord. If they have persecuted me, they will also persecute you; if they have kept my saying, they will keep yours also."

John 15:19-20, KJV

You also died to the law through the body of Christ, that you might belong to another, to him who was raised from the dead, in order that we might bear fruit to God.

Romans 7:4, NIV

Know that the LORD, he is God! It is he who made us, and we are his; we are his people, and the sheep of his pasture.

Psalm 100:3, ESV

In him we were also chosen, having been predestined according to the plan of him who works out everything in conformity with the purpose of his will, in order that we, who were the first to hope in Christ, might be for the praise of his glory.

Ephesians 1:11-12, NIV

You whom I took from the ends of the earth, and called from its farthest corners, saying to you, "You are my servant, I have chosen you and not cast you off"; fear not, for I am with you; be not dismayed, for I am your God; I will strengthen you, I will help you, I will uphold you with my righteous right hand.

Isaiah 41:9-10, ESV

We ought always to thank God for you, brothers loved by the Lord, because from the beginning God chose you to be saved through the sanctifying work of the Spirit and through belief in the truth.

2 Thessalonians 2:13, NIV

We are God's workmanship, created in Christ Jesus to do good works, which God prepared in advance for us to do.

Ephesians 2:10, NIV

Put on then, as God's chosen ones, holy and beloved, compassion, kindness, humility, meekness, and patience.

Colossians 3:12, ESV

Blessed be the God and Father of our Lord Jesus Christ, who has blessed us with every spiritual blessing in the heavenly places in Christ, just as He chose us in Him before the foundation of the world, that we should be holy and without blame before Him in love, having predestined us to adoption as sons by Jesus Christ to Himself, according to the good pleasure of His will.

Ephesians 1:3-5, NKJV

"You did not choose me, but I chose you and appointed you that you should go and bear fruit and that your fruit should abide, so that whatever you ask the Father in my name, he may give it to you."

John 15:16, ESV

CHURCH

And let the peace of Christ rule in your hearts, to which indeed you were called in one body.

Colossians 3:15, ESV

Christ's body was broken for us and He died and rose again that He might impart the life of God to the souls of men, and God began to give His Son another body, the Spiritual body of Christ, the Church, of which Christ is the Head and Lord. By God's infinite grace we who read this have doubtless been born of God and made to be a member of Christ's spiritual body.

If we have been saved by God's grace then we are truly members of His body, and that being so, we are to be careful to be healthy members, fulfilling our function and contributing to the health of the whole body. This is possible as we live in living touch with the Head, from whom we receive both our life and our instruction, and being in right relation to Him we are adjusted in true fellowship with all others who are also members of His body.

The Word's view

on the church

"And I tell you, you are Peter, and on this rock I will build my church, and the gates of hell shall not prevail against it."

Matthew 16:18, ESV

Now therefore ye are no more strangers and foreigners, but fellowcitizens with the saints, and of the household of God; And are built upon the foundation of the apostles and prophets, Jesus Christ himself being the chief corner stone; In whom all the building fitly framed together groweth unto an holy temple in the Lord: In whom ye also are builded together for an habitation of God through the Spirit.

Ephesians 2:19-22, KJV

You are the body of Christ, and members individually. And God has appointed these in the church: first apostles, second prophets, third teachers, after that miracles, then gifts of healings, helps, administrations, varieties of tongues.

1 Corinthians 12:27-28, NKJV

Know ye not that your body is the temple of the Holy Ghost which is in you, which ye have of God, and ye are not your own?

1 Corinthians 6:19, KJV

For as the body is one and has many members, but all the members of that one body, being many, are one body, so also is Christ. For by one Spirit we were all baptized into one body – whether Jews or Greeks, whether slaves or free – and have all been made to drink into one Spirit. For in fact the body is not one member but many.

1 Corinthians 12:12-14 NKJV

For as in one body we have many members, and the members do not all have the same function, so we, though many, are one body in Christ, and individually members one of another.

Romans 12:4-5, ESV

And he is the head of the body, the church. He is the beginning, the firstborn from the dead, that in everything he might be preeminent.

Colossians 1:18, ESV

It was he who gave some to be apostles, some to be prophets, some to be evangelists, and some to be pastors and teachers, to prepare God's people for works of service, so that the body of Christ may be built up until we all reach unity in the faith and in the knowledge of the Son of God and become mature, attaining to the whole measure of the fullness of Christ.

Ephesians 4:11-13, NIV

His intent was that now, through the church, the manifold wisdom of God should be made known to the rulers and authorities in the heavenly realms, according to his eternal purpose which he accomplished in Christ Jesus our Lord. In him and through faith in him we may approach God with freedom and confidence.

Ephesians 3:10-12, NIV

"And I have other sheep that are not of this fold. I must bring them also, and they will listen to my voice. So there will be one flock, one shepherd."

John 10:16, ESV

Comfort

May our Lord Jesus Christ himself and God our Father, who loved us and by his grace gave us eternal encouragement and good hope, encourage your hearts and strengthen you in every good deed and word.

2 Thessalonians 2:16-17, NIV

Sadness and sorrow are an indisputable reality in human life. How well do we not know that! That is why it is such a glorious comfort to remember the words of the Lord Himself: *"I will ask the Father and He will give you another Counselor to be with you forever – the Spirit of truth"* (Jn. 14:16, NIV). In the midst of our adversity and sickness, our poverty and lack, our cares and worries, Someone who understands and cares comes to us with these words: *"Blessed are those who mourn, because they will be comforted"* (Mt. 5:4, NIV).

Not far from Marah with its bitter waters is Elim with its twelve fountains and many palm trees. Trust God to lead you from Marah to Elim by His understanding and loving grace.

Comfort from
the Word

Yea, though I walk through the valley of the shadow of death, I will fear no evil: for thou art with me; thy rod and thy staff they comfort me.

Psalm 23:4, KJV

Praise be to the God and Father of our Lord Jesus Christ, the Father of compassion and the God of all comfort, who comforts us in all our troubles, so that we can comfort those in any trouble with the comfort we ourselves have received from God.

2 Corinthians 1:3-4, NIV

"But the Comforter, which is the Holy Ghost, whom the Father will send in my name, he shall teach you all things, and bring all things to your remembrance, whatsoever I have said unto you."

John 14:26, KJV

Wait on the LORD: be of good courage, and he shall strengthen thine heart: wait, I say, on the LORD.

Psalm 27:14, KJV

You who have made me see many troubles and calamities will revive me again; from the depths of the earth you will bring me up again. You will increase my greatness and comfort me again.

Psalm 71:20-21, ESV

God is our refuge and strength, a very present help in trouble. Therefore will not we fear, though the earth be removed, and though the mountains be carried into the midst of the sea; Though the waters thereof roar and be troubled, though the mountains shake with the swelling thereof.

Psalm 46:1-3, KJV

Though I walk in the midst of trouble, you preserve my life; you stretch out your hand against the wrath of my enemies, and your right hand delivers me.

Psalm 138:7, ESV

The LORD is good, a stronghold in the day of trouble; and He knows those who trust in Him.

Nahum 1:7, NKJV

"As one whom his mother comforteth, so will I comfort you."

Isaiah 66:13, KJV

The LORD is my rock and my fortress and my deliverer; My God, my strength, in whom I will trust; My shield and the horn of my salvation, my stronghold.

Psalm 18:2, NKJV

Just as the sufferings of Christ flow over into our lives, so also through Christ our comfort overflows.

2 Corinthians 1:5, NIV

For the LORD will not cast off forever, but, though he cause grief, he will have compassion according to the abundance of his steadfast love; for he does not willingly afflict or grieve the children of men.

Lamentations 3:31-33, ESV

Thou hast enlarged my steps under me, that my feet did not slip. For who is God save the LORD? or who is a rock save our God? It is God that girdeth me with strength, and maketh my way perfect.

Psalm 18:36, 31-32, KJV

$\mathcal{D}$ESPAIR

Be of good courage, and He shall strengthen your heart, all you who hope in the LORD.

Psalm 31:24, *NKJV*

It was Dostoevsky who said that our hosannas must continually be heard through the whirlwinds of disappointment. These very whirlwinds have a lot to do with the intense bitterness that sometimes overcomes you.

For he who dwells in the dark shadows of great disappointment, there is often nothing left but faith in God. He may rant and rave in protest against this faith, even as Job did with all his taunts and questions, but faith doesn't come without strife. It's good for the draining of the wound. But eventually the process ends. It doesn't mean that he suddenly strikes up with a cheery new song because his disappointments have been instantly changed into blessings, but that he rather rests in the knowledge that while he may be able to do without just about everything else, he cannot do without God in his life, because without God, there is nothing.

COMFORT

IN DESPAIR

Uphold me according to your promise, that I may live, and let me not be put to shame in my hope!

Psalm 119:116, ESV

For this is what the high and lofty One says – he who lives forever, whose name is holy: "I live in a high and holy place, but also with him who is contrite and lowly in spirit, to revive the spirit of the lowly and to revive the heart of the contrite."

Isaiah 57:15, NIV

They who wait for the LORD shall renew their strength; they shall mount up with wings like eagles; they shall run and not be weary; they shall walk and not faint.

Isaiah 40:31, ESV

Attend unto my cry; for I am brought very low: deliver me from my persecutors; for they are stronger than I.

Psalm 142:6, KJV

For the LORD loves justice; he will not forsake his saints. They are preserved forever.

Psalm 37:28, ESV

Ah Lord GOD! behold, thou hast made the heaven and the earth by thy great power and stretched out arm, and there is nothing too hard for thee.

Jeremiah 32:17, KJV

Why art thou cast down, O my soul? and why art thou disquieted within me? hope thou in God: for I shall yet praise him, who is the health of my countenance, and my God.

Psalm 42:11, KJV

Therefore we do not lose heart. Even though our outward man is perishing, yet the inward man is being renewed day by day. For our light affliction, which is but for a moment, is working for us a far more exceeding and eternal weight of glory, while we do not look at the things which are seen, but at the things which are not seen. For the things which are seen are temporary, but the things which are not seen are eternal.

2 Corinthians 4:16-18, NKJV

He giveth power to the faint; and to them that have no might he increaseth strength.

Isaiah 40:29, KJV

"Fear not, for I have redeemed you; I have called you by your name; You are Mine."

Isaiah 43:1, NKJV

We know that in all things God works for the good of those who love him, who have been called according to his purpose.

Romans 8:28, NIV

The LORD shall fight for you, and ye shall hold your peace.

Exodus 14:14, KJV

Wait for the LORD; be strong, and let your heart take courage; wait for the LORD!

Psalm 27:14, ESV

"The LORD is my portion," says my soul, "therefore I will hope in him." The LORD is good to those who wait for him, to the soul who seeks him. It is good that one should wait quietly for the salvation of the LORD.

Lamentations 3:24-26, ESV

$\mathcal{D}$ISAPPOINTED

*The LORD is close to the brokenhearted and saves
those who are crushed in spirit.*

Psalm 34:18, NIV

Anyone who lives long enough will be
disappointed. Life seems to conspire to
let us down at crucial moments. Many of
our hopes and aspirations seem to wash up
as flotsam on the shores of broken dreams.
Yet the Bible assures us that God's plans for
our lives will be fulfilled. His thoughts do
not fail. All things are possible with Him,
because He is able to do all things.

When you are dealing with a disappointment, it seems insensitive to suggest
that God allowed the events to unfold as they
did because of His greater plan and purpose
for your life. And yet that is the truth. The
way to glory was, for Jesus, through the
cross. He was crucified, but He overcame
death and offers you that hope as an anchor
for your soul.

Encouragement for

the disappointed

And the LORD, he it is that doth go before thee; he will be with thee, he will not fail thee, neither forsake thee: fear not, neither be dismayed.

Deuteronomy 31:8, KJV

But Jesus looked at them and said, "With man this is impossible, but with God all things are possible."

Matthew 19:26, ESV

Jesus said to him, "If you can believe, all things are possible to him who believes." Immediately the father of the child cried out and said with tears, "Lord, I believe; help my unbelief!"

Mark 9:23-24, NKJV

Now to Him who is able to do exceedingly abundantly above all that we ask or think, according to the power that works in us, to Him be glory in the church by Christ Jesus to all generations, forever and ever.

Ephesians 3:20-21, NKJV

Many are the afflictions of the righteous: but the LORD delivereth him out of them all.

Psalm 34:19, KJV

"If you remain in me and my words remain in you, ask whatever you wish, and it will be given you."

John 15:7, NIV

My flesh and my heart faileth: but God is the strength of my heart, and my portion for ever.

Psalm 73:26, KJV

"Come to Me, all you who labor and are heavy laden, and I will give you rest. Take My yoke upon you and learn from Me, for I am gentle and lowly in heart, and you will find rest for your souls. For My yoke is easy and My burden is light."

Matthew 11:28-30, NKJV

Let us then with confidence draw near to the throne of grace, that we may receive mercy and find grace to help in time of need.

Hebrews 4:16, ESV

Why are you cast down, O my soul, and why are you in turmoil within me? Hope in God; for I shall again praise him, my salvation and my God.

Psalm 42:11, ESV

The Spirit also helps in our weaknesses. For we do not know what we should pray for as we ought, but the Spirit Himself makes intercession for us with groanings which cannot be uttered. Now He who searches the hearts knows what the mind of the Spirit is, because He makes intercession for the saints according to the will of God.

Romans 8:26-27, NKJV

Draw near to God, and he will draw near to you. Cleanse your hands, you sinners, and purify your hearts, you double-minded. Humble yourselves before the Lord, and he will exalt you.

James 4:8, 10, ESV

The sacrifices of God are a broken spirit: a broken and a contrite heart, O God, thou wilt not despise.

Psalm 51:17, KJV

*D*ISCOURAGED

Be of good courage, and he shall strengthen your heart, all ye that hope in the LORD.
Psalm 31:24, KJV

People often feel that they cannot go one step further. The pressure and worries of daily life start to take their toll. Lack of appreciation makes people feel like throwing in the towel! While it is good, right, and courteous for people to appreciate your input, lack of acknowledgement should never be used as an excuse for giving up. Your main goal in life should always be to please God and seek His approval. If you complete your daily duties with this attitude, you will be a true servant of the Lord.

No matter how despondent you feel, never forget that Jesus is with you in everything you undertake. In the most depressing circumstances, remember His example: He was victorious through all kinds of discouragement and oppression – even death on the cross. When you are tempted to give up, turn to your Savior. In Him you will find the inspiration to carry on.

Hope for

THE DISCOURAGED

"I will make them strong in the LORD, and they shall walk in his name," declares the LORD.

Zechariah 10:12, ESV

LORD, thou hast heard the desire of the humble: thou wilt prepare their heart, thou wilt cause thine ear to hear.

Psalm 10:17, KJV

But you, O LORD, are a shield about me, my glory, and the lifter of my head.

Psalm 3:3, ESV

Cast your cares on the LORD and he will sustain you; he will never let the righteous fall.

Psalm 55:22, NIV

I know whom I have believed, and am convinced that he is able to guard what I have entrusted to him for that day.

2 Timothy 1:12, NIV

For I know that my redeemer liveth, and that he shall stand at the latter day upon the earth.

Job 19:25, KJV

In this you rejoice, though now for a little while, as was necessary, you have been grieved by various trials, so that the tested genuineness of your faith – more precious than gold that perishes though it is tested by fire – may be found to result in praise and glory and honor at the revelation of Jesus Christ.

1 Peter 1:6-7, ESV

Let your conversation be without covetousness; and be content with such things as ye have: for he hath said, I will never leave thee, nor forsake thee. So that we may boldly say, The Lord is my helper, and I will not fear what man shall do unto me.

Hebrews 13:5-6, KJV

Is anything too hard for the LORD?

Genesis 18:14, NIV

Sing praise to the LORD, you saints of His, and give thanks at the remembrance of His holy name. For His anger is but for a moment, His favor is for life; Weeping may endure for a night, but joy comes in the morning.

Psalm 30:4-5, NKJV

The LORD is a stronghold for the oppressed, a stronghold in times of trouble. And those who know your name put their trust in you, for you, O LORD, have not forsaken those who seek you.

Psalm 9:9-10, ESV

I saw the LORD always before me. Because he is at my right hand, I will not be shaken.

Psalm 16:8, NIV

As ye have therefore received Christ Jesus the Lord, so walk ye in him: Rooted and built up in him, and established in the faith, as ye have been taught, abounding therein with thanksgiving.

Colossians 2:6-7, KJV

Let the LORD be magnified, who has pleasure in the prosperity of His servant.

Psalm 35:27, NKJV

Everything that was written in the past was written to teach us, so that through endurance and the encouragement of the Scriptures we might have hope.

Romans 15:4, NIV

ETERNAL LIFE

Jesus said to her, "I am the resurrection and the life. Whoever believes in me, though he die, yet shall he live, and everyone who lives and believes in me shall never die. Do you believe this?"

John 11:25-26, ESV

The life which is of God was brought to earth by the Son of God and in the Incarnation was united to the life of man, and revealed and expressed in a human body in human life. After that, the Son died and rose again and the life and immortality became available for men. The Son has life in Himself and gives it to those who believe, so that the same life, divine and eternal, is our life and because He lives we live also.

This new life in Christ is eternal. It will not only be our portion here but will be our privileged possession when the call comes from heaven and we pass into the eternity from which Christ brought the life in the first instance. He lives forever and ever and so shall we because we are indwelt and possessed by the same everlasting life.

God's promise
of Eternal Life

"Do not labor for the food which perishes, but for the food which endures to everlasting life, which the Son of Man will give you."

John 6:27, NKJV

But now that you have been set free from sin and have become slaves to God, the benefit you reap leads to holiness, and the result is eternal life. For the wages of sin is death, but the gift of God is eternal life in Christ Jesus our Lord.

Romans 6:22-23, NIV

"And this is the will of him that sent me, that every one which seeth the Son, and believeth on him, may have everlasting life: and I will raise him up at the last day."

John 6:40, KJV

For the one who sows to his own flesh will from the flesh reap corruption, but the one who sows to the Spirit will from the Spirit reap eternal life.

Galatians 6:8, ESV

"Truly, truly, I say to you, whoever believes has eternal life."

John 6:47, ESV

"But whosoever drinketh of the water that I shall give him shall never thirst; but the water that I shall give him shall be in him a well of water springing up into everlasting life."

John 4:14, KJV

"He that believeth on the Son hath everlasting life."

John 3:36, KJV

How great are his signs! and how mighty are his wonders! his kingdom is an everlasting kingdom, and his dominion is from generation to generation.

Daniel 4:3, KJV

"For God so loved the world that he gave his one and only Son, that whoever believes in him shall not perish but have eternal life."

John 3:16, NIV

The one who sows to please the Spirit, from the Spirit will reap eternal life.

Galatians 6:8, NIV

And this is the testimony, that God gave us eternal life, and this life is in his Son. Whoever has the Son has life.

1 John 5:11-12, ESV

If what you heard from the beginning abides in you, you also will abide in the Son and in the Father. And this is the promise that He has promised us – eternal life.

1 John 2:24-25, NKJV

If you confess with your mouth, "Jesus is Lord," and believe in your heart that God raised him from the dead, you will be saved. For it is with your heart that you believe and are justified, and it is with your mouth that you confess and are saved.

Romans 10:9-10, NIV

"In my Father's house are many mansions: if it were not so, I would have told you. I go to prepare a place for you. And if I go and prepare a place for you, I will come again, and receive you unto myself; that where I am, there ye may be also."

John 14:2-3, KJV

$\mathcal{F}$AITH

Trust in the LORD with all your heart, and lean not on your own understanding; in all your ways acknowledge Him, and He shall direct your paths.

Proverbs 3:5-6, NKJV

Many people have great difficulty in exercising their faith when they face a serious problem. When our faith is being tested, we are inclined to fall back on what we know, rather than to trust God to carry us through.

A study of God's holy Word reveals countless examples of those people who put their steadfast trust in God. And for this they received their reward in Christ Jesus. God wonderfully met their needs according to the riches of His grace. This was especially true in the life of Jesus Christ. The classic example of this is the arrest, death, resurrection and ascension of our Savior. His love for God was so certain that He could say with assurance, *"nevertheless, not as will, but as You will"* (Mt. 26:39, NIV). Tru God steadfastly. Find your strength in t Holy Spirit. And you will be rewarded w His perfect will is revealed in your lif

PROMISES

OF FAITH

You will seek the LORD your God and you will find him, if you search after him with all your heart and with all your soul.

Deuteronomy 4:29, ESV

Jesus said to him, "Have you believed because you have seen me? Blessed are those who have not seen and yet have believed."

John 20:29, ESV

Faith comes from hearing the message, and the message is heard through the word of Christ.

Romans 10:17, NIV

"Lord, I believe; help my unbelief!"

Mark 9:24, NKJV

"I tell you, whatever you ask in prayer, believe that you have received it, and it will be yours."

Mark 11:24, ESV

Jesus stood up and cried out, "If anyone thirsts, let him come to me and drink. Whoever believes in me, as the Scripture has said, 'Out of his heart will flow rivers of living water.'"

John 7:37-38, ESV

"Blessed is the man who trusts in the LORD, and whose hope is the LORD. For he shall be like a tree planted by the waters, which spreads out its roots by the river, and will not fear when heat comes."

Jeremiah 17:7-8, NKJV

It is no longer I who live, but Christ who lives in me. And the life I now live in the flesh I live by faith.

Galatians 2:20, ESV

For by grace you have been saved through faith. And this is not your own doing; it is the gift of God.

Ephesians 2:8, ESV

Faith is being sure of what we hope for and certain of what we do not see.

Hebrews 11:1, NIV

In all circumstances take up the shield of faith, with which you can extinguish all the flaming darts of the evil one.

Ephesians 6:16, ESV

Jesus answered and said, Verily I say unto you, if ye have faith, and doubt not, ye shall not only do this which is done to the fig tree, but also if ye shall say unto this mountain, be thou removed, and be thou cast into the sea; it shall be done. And all things, whatsoever ye shall ask in prayer, believing, ye shall receive.

Matthew 21:21-22, KJV

For I am not ashamed of the gospel, for it is the power of God for salvation to everyone who believes, to the Jew first and also to the Greek. For in it the righteousness of God is revealed from faith for faith, as it is written, "The righteous shall live by faith."

Romans 1:16-17, ESV

But now a righteousness from God, apart from law, has been made known, to which the Law and the Prophets testify. This righteousness from God comes through faith in Jesus Christ to all who believe.

Romans 3:21-22, NIV

FEAR

When I am afraid, I put my trust in you. In God, whose word I praise, in God I trust; I shall not be afraid. What can flesh do to me?

Psalm 56:3-4, ESV

Fear has a very destructive effect on our lives. Even though fear is often linked with physical danger, its effects are far wider than physical illness. Much damage can be inflicted on your nervous system and emotional well-being because of the tension and stress caused by fear.

The only way to rid yourself of fear and to solve the problems of its effect is to cling to God and His love. His promise never to leave you or forsake you, remains steadfast. Through Christ, God expelled all need for fear from our lives. Christ overcame the anguish of death, therefore you can trust Him to lead you out of the jungle of fear so that you will be able to handle whatever comes your way in His power and strength. Draw on the courage and trust that He gives you and you will live victoriously in every situation.

From fear

to faith

The LORD is my light and my salvation; whom shall I fear? The LORD is the strength of my life; of whom shall I be afraid? When the wicked came against me to eat up my flesh, my enemies and foes, they stumbled and fell. Though an army may encamp against me, my heart shall not fear; though war may rise against me, in this I will be confident.

Psalm 27:1-3, NKJV

Have not I commanded thee? Be strong and of a good courage; be not afraid, neither be thou dismayed: for the LORD thy God is with thee whithersoever thou goest.

Joshua 1:9, KJV

"Fear not, for I have redeemed you; I have summoned you by name; you are mine. When you pass through the waters, I will be with you; and when you pass through the rivers, they will not sweep over you."

Isaiah 43:1-2, NIV

I lift up my eyes to the hills – where does my help come from? My help comes from the LORD, the Maker of heaven and earth. He will not let your foot slip – he who watches over you will not slumber; indeed, he who watches over Israel will neither slumber nor sleep. The LORD watches over you – the LORD is your shade at your right hand; the sun will not harm you by day, nor the moon by night. The LORD will keep you from all harm – he will watch over your life; the LORD will watch over your coming and going both now and forevermore.

Psalm 121:1-8, NIV

Even though I walk through the valley of the shadow of death, I will fear no evil, for you are with me; your rod and your staff, they comfort me.

Psalm 23:4, ESV

And the LORD, he it is that doth go before thee; he will be with thee, he will not fail thee, neither forsake thee: fear not, neither be dismayed.

Deuteronomy 31:8, KJV

Thou shalt not be afraid for the terror by night; nor for the arrow that flieth by day; Nor for the pestilence that walketh in darkness; nor for the destruction that wasteth at noonday. There shall no evil befall thee, neither shall any plague come nigh thy dwelling. For he shall give his angels charge over thee, to keep thee in all thy ways.

Psalm 91:5-6, 10-11, KJV

Fear thou not; for I am with thee: be not dismayed; for I am thy God: I will strengthen thee; yea, I will help thee; yea, I will uphold thee with the right hand of my righteousness.

Isaiah 41:10, KJV

Do not be afraid of sudden terror or of the ruin of the wicked when it comes, for the LORD will be your confidence and will keep your foot from being caught.

Proverbs 3:25-26, ESV

"Peace I leave with you, My peace I give to you; not as the world gives do I give to you. Let not your heart be troubled, neither let it be afraid."

John 14:27, NKJV

$\mathcal{F}$ORGIVENESS

If we confess our sins, he is faithful and just and will forgive us our sins and purify us from all un-righteousness.

1 John 1:9, NIV

For men who are conscious of having sinned against a holy God, for all whose consciences are burdened with a load of guilt, there can never be a sweeter sound than that of pardon. To hear and to believe that the holy God whom we have so grievously offended, has sent the message of a full and free forgiveness, is to make the heart glad.

There is no sinner too vile to be pardoned and there is none so righteous as not to need it. Though our sins be of the most heinous kind they can be completely forgiven and removed, because it is God who forgives.

If we are Christians we have already experienced this great joy, but does the fact of our pardon still make us wonder and worship? And does the wonder of it still move us and make us witnesses to others who have never heard the good news?

GOD'S PROMISES

OF FORGIVENESS

In Him we have redemption through His blood, the forgiveness of sins, according to the riches of His grace.

Ephesians 1:7, NKJV

And Peter said to them, "Repent and be baptized every one of you in the name of Jesus Christ for the forgiveness of your sins, and you will receive the gift of the Holy Spirit."

Acts 2:38, ESV

All the prophets testify about him that everyone who believes in him receives forgiveness of sins through his name.

Acts 10:43, NIV

"And forgive us our sins; for we also forgive every one that is indebted to us. And lead us not into temptation; but deliver us from evil."

Luke 11:4, KJV

"The Son of man hath power upon earth to forgive sins."

Luke 5:24, KJV

Therefore, as God's chosen people, holy and dearly loved, clothe yourselves with compassion, kindness, humility, gentleness and patience. Bear with each other and forgive whatever grievances you may have against one another. Forgive as the Lord forgave you.

Colossians 3:12-13, NIV

If my people, which are called by my name, shall humble themselves, and pray, and seek my face, and turn from their wicked ways; then will I hear from heaven, and will forgive their sin, and will heal their land.

2 Chronicles 7:14, KJV

As far as the east is from the west, so far has He removed our transgressions from us.

Psalm 103:12, NKJV

I, even I, am he that blotteth out thy transgressions for mine own sake, and will not remember thy sins.

Isaiah 43:25, KJV

He will again have compassion on us; he will tread our iniquities under foot. You will cast all our sins into the depths of the sea.

Micah 7:19, ESV

"Come now, let us reason together," says the LORD. "Though your sins are like scarlet, they shall be as white as snow; though they are red as crimson, they shall be like wool."

Isaiah 1:18, NIV

"For if you forgive men their trespasses, your heavenly Father will also forgive you. But if you do not forgive men their trespasses, neither will your Father forgive your trespasses."

Matthew 6:14-15, NKJV

Have mercy upon me, O God, according to Your lovingkindness; according to the multitude of Your tender mercies, blot out my transgressions. Wash me thoroughly from my iniquity, and cleanse me from my sin.

Psalm 51:1-2, NKJV

Therefore, my brothers, I want you to know that through Jesus the forgiveness of sins is proclaimed to you. Through him everyone who believes is justified from everything you could not be justified from by the law of Moses.

Acts 13:38-39, NIV

GOD'S WILL

"Call to me and I will answer you and tell you great and unsearchable things you do not know."

Jeremiah 33:3, NIV

You have to search for God's will for your life in order to have a positive goal. With Christ in control of your life, you will stop drifting around aimlessly and become an inspired and positive Christian.

The renewal of your spiritual experience starts when you invite Christ into your life and open yourself up to the working of the Holy Spirit allowing Him to take control of your thoughts and actions. Then you discover that as you are living in harmony with Him, new areas of service are revealed to you. You realize that you are being led by the Holy Spirit into spheres of life which you had not even considered before.

When you have a feeling that God is guiding you, you need to confirm it in prayer. Be courageous, act confidently and trust steadfastly in God. To discover God's will for your life not only requires faith, but positive action as well.

GUIDANCE
INTO GOD'S WILL

Do not be conformed to this world, but be transformed by the renewing of your mind, that you may prove what is that good and acceptable and perfect will of God.

Romans 12:2, NKJV

Thus saith the LORD, Stand ye in the ways, and see, and ask for the old paths, where is the good way, and walk therein, and ye shall find rest for your souls.

Jeremiah 6:16, KJV

He made known to us the mystery of his will according to his good pleasure, which he purposed in Christ, to be put into effect when the times will have reached their fulfillment – to bring all things in heaven and on earth together under one head, even Christ.

Ephesians 1:9-10, NIV

"Now we know that God heareth not sinners: but if any man be a worshipper of God, and doeth his will, him he heareth."

John 9:31, KJV

For this is the will of God, that by doing good you may put to silence the ignorance of foolish men.

1 Peter 2:15, NKJV

In him we have obtained an inheritance, having been predestined according to the purpose of him who works all things according to the counsel of his will.

Ephesians 1:11, ESV

It is God's will that you should be sanctified.

1 Thessalonians 4:3, NIV

"You will seek me and find me. When you seek me with all your heart, I will be found by you," declares the LORD.

Jeremiah 29:13-14, ESV

The world is passing away, and the lust of it; but he who does the will of God abides forever.

1 John 2:17, NKJV

Trust in the LORD with all your heart, and do not lean on your own understanding. In all your ways acknowledge him, and he will make straight your paths.

Proverbs 3:5-6, ESV

He who searches our hearts knows the mind of the Spirit, because the Spirit intercedes for the saints in accordance with God's will. And we know that in all things God works for the good of those who love him.

Romans 8:27-28, NIV

One thing I do, forgetting those things which are behind and reaching forward to those things which are ahead, I press toward the goal for the prize of the upward call of God in Christ Jesus.

Philippians 3:13-14, NKJV

Give thanks in all circumstances, for this is God's will for you in Christ Jesus.

1 Thessalonians 5:18, NIV

"For I know the plans I have for you," declares the LORD, "plans to prosper you and not to harm you, plans to give you hope and a future."

Jeremiah 29:11, NIV

We have not ceased to pray for you, asking that you may be filled with the knowledge of his will in all spiritual wisdom and understanding.

Colossians 1:9, ESV

GRACE

It is by grace you have been saved, through faith – and this not from yourselves, it is the gift of God.

Ephesians 2:8, NIV

Where would we have been if it were not for the grace of God? One of our best-loved songs speaks of "amazing grace". This song speaks of a redeeming God whose love is so great that He gave His all through grace.

While you meditate on Christ's sacrifice, you are confronted with the highest deed of compassion and love that this world has ever known – that the Son of God took your guilt and mine upon Himself and sacrificed His life in order to redeem us from sin.

But His grace extends further than that. We are untrustworthy and forgetful and often turn away from God. Yet Christ waits patiently and lovingly for us to return to Him. Through His love He guides us back to the road of obedience and love.

You can express your gratitude for His boundless love by expressing to others the same grace and mercy that Jesus has bestowed upon you.

THE GIFT

OF GRACE

The LORD your God is gracious and merciful, and will not turn away his face from you, if ye return unto him.

2 Chronicles 30:9, KJV

Every good gift and every perfect gift is from above, and comes down from the Father of lights.

James 1:17, NKJV

And of his fullness have all we received, and grace for grace. For the law was given by Moses, but grace and truth came by Jesus Christ.

John 1:16-17, KJV

For the LORD God is a sun and shield: the LORD will give grace and glory: no good thing will he withhold from them that walk uprightly.

Psalm 84:11, KJV

To each one of us grace was given according to the measure of Christ's gift.

Ephesians 4:7, NKJV

For the grace of God has appeared, bringing salvation for all people, training us to renounce ungodliness and worldly passions, and to live self-controlled, upright, and godly lives in the present age.

Titus 2:11-12, ESV

For all have sinned, and come short of the glory of God; Being justified freely by his grace through the redemption that is in Christ Jesus.

Romans 3:23-24, KJV

He said to me, "My grace is sufficient for you, for My strength is made perfect in weakness." Therefore most gladly I will rather boast in my infirmities, that the power of Christ may rest upon me.

2 Corinthians 12:9, NKJV

Surely he scorneth the scorners: but he giveth grace unto the lowly.

Proverbs 3:34, KJV

Who is a God like you, who pardons sin and forgives the transgression of the remnant of his inheritance? You do not stay angry forever but delight to show mercy.

Micah 7:18, NIV

Therefore the LORD waits to be gracious to you, and therefore he exalts himself to show mercy to you. For the LORD is a God of justice; blessed are those who wait for him.

Isaiah 30:18, ESV

He saved us, not because of righteous things we had done, but because of his mercy. He saved us through the washing of rebirth and renewal by the Holy Spirit, whom he poured out on us through Jesus Christ, so that, having been justified by his grace, we might become heirs having the hope of eternal life.

Titus 3:5-7, NIV

In Him we have redemption through His blood, the forgiveness of sins, according to the riches of His grace which He made to abound toward us in all wisdom and prudence.

Ephesians 1:7-8, NKJV

We believe it is through the grace of our Lord Jesus that we are saved.

Acts 15:11, NIV

But grow in the grace and knowledge of our Lord and Savior Jesus Christ.

2 Peter 3:18, ESV

GUIDANCE

Whether you turn to the right or to the left, your ears will hear a voice behind you, saying, "This is the way; walk in it."

Isaiah 30:21, NIV

It is a blessed assurance to know that you are guided, from day to day, by an omnipotent and loving God. The Lord does not promise that all the pastures will always be green: sometimes they are barren and sterile and desolate. He has also not promised that the waters will always be tranquil: sometimes the waves break turbulently over us and the sky above is covered with ominous storm clouds. But if we put our childlike and unconditional trust in Him, we may rest assured that He will guide us in our everyday lives.

We must stay close to the Shepherd in order to be guided by Him. Often we experience difficult and incomprehensible times, sometimes even storm and stress. Regardless of how stormy and unpredictable the circumstances of our lives may be, our spirit will be quiet and peaceful if we allow Him to be our Governor.

GUIDANCE
FROM THE WORD

I will instruct you and teach you in the way
you should go; I will guide you with My eye.

Psalm 32:8, NKJV

Again Jesus spoke to them, saying, "I am
the light of the world. Whoever follows me
will not walk in darkness, but will have the
light of life."

John 8:12, ESV

If any of you lacks wisdom, he should ask
God, who gives generously to all without
finding fault, and it will be given to him.
But when he asks, he must believe and not
doubt.

James 1:5-6, NIV

Listen to my instruction and be wise; do not
ignore it. Blessed is the man who listens to
me, watching daily at my doors, waiting at
my doorway.

Proverbs 8:33-34, NIV

Hear counsel, and receive instruction, that
thou mayest be wise in thy latter end.

Proverbs 19:20, KJV

The steps of a good man are ordered by the LORD, and He delights in his way. Though he fall, he shall not be utterly cast down; for the LORD upholds him with His hand.

Psalm 37:23-24, NKJV

For this God is our God for ever and ever: he will be our guide even unto death.

Psalm 48:14, KJV

Trust in the LORD with all your heart, and lean not on your own understanding; in all your ways acknowledge Him, and He shall direct your paths.

Proverbs 3:5-6, NKJV

Yet I am always with you; you hold me by my right hand. You guide me with your counsel, and afterward you will take me into glory.

Psalm 73:23-24, NIV

The humble He guides in justice, and the humble He teaches His way.

Psalm 25:9, NKJV

A man's heart deviseth his way: but the LORD directeth his steps.

Proverbs 16:9, KJV

He makes me lie down in green pastures, he leads me beside quiet waters, he restores my soul. He guides me in paths of righteousness for his name's sake.

Psalm 23:2-3, NIV

"When the Spirit of truth comes, he will guide you into all the truth, for he will not speak on his own authority, but whatever he hears he will speak, and he will declare to you the things that are to come."

John 16:13, ESV

He brought his people out like a flock; he led them like sheep through the desert. He guided them safely, so they were unafraid.

Psalm 78:52-53, NIV

For as many as are led by the Spirit of God, they are the sons of God.

Romans 8:14, KJV

"Call to Me, and I will answer you, and show you great and mighty things, which you do not know."

Jeremiah 33:3, NKJV

*H*EAVEN

In my Father's house are many rooms. If it were not so, would I have told you that I go to prepare a place for you? And if I go and prepare a place for you, I will come again and will take you to myself, that where I am you may be also.

John 14:2-3, ESV

Christians have the assurance that the life we are living on this earth is not all the life we will ever have! We will live for ever in heaven with God. This glorious truth sustains us when we walk through deep, dark valleys. And we are encouraged to ensure that all we do on earth prepares us for the life we will live for eternity. We lay up for ourselves eternal treasures, because of the hope of glory that we have been promised.

How much easier it is to endure difficulties in daily life when we measure them against the vastness and splendor of eternity with God. Let us look with longing to the day when all tears will be wiped away and we will see God face to face in heaven.

THE PROMISE

OF HEAVEN

Thy kingdom is an everlasting kingdom, and thy dominion endureth throughout all generations.

Psalm 145:13, KJV

"Lay up for yourselves treasures in heaven, where neither moth nor rust destroys and where thieves do not break in and steal. For where your treasure is, there your heart will be also."

Matthew 6:20-21, NKJV

"Therefore whoever confesses Me before men, him I will also confess before My Father who is in heaven."

Matthew 10:32, NKJV

The Lord himself will come down from heaven, with a loud command, with the voice of the archangel and with the trumpet call of God, and the dead in Christ will rise first. After that, we who are still alive and are left will be caught up together with them in the clouds to meet the Lord in the air. And so we will be with the Lord forever.

1 Thessalonians 4:16-17, NKJV

But our citizenship is in heaven, and from it we await a Savior, the Lord Jesus Christ, who will transform our lowly body to be like his glorious body, by the power that enables him even to subject all things to himself.

Philippians 3:20-21, ESV

I saw a new heaven and a new earth, for the first heaven and the first earth had passed away. Also there was no more sea. Then I, John, saw the holy city, New Jerusalem, coming down out of heaven from God, prepared as a bride adorned for her husband. And I heard a loud voice from heaven saying, "Behold, the tabernacle of God is with men, and He will dwell with them, and they shall be His people. God Himself will be with them and be their God. And God will wipe away every tear from their eyes; there shall be no more death, nor sorrow, nor crying. There shall be no more pain, for the former things have passed away."

Revelation 21:1-4, NKJV

Hear from heaven, your dwelling place, and when you hear, forgive.

1 Kings 8:30, NIV

"Then the King will say to those on his right, 'Come, you who are blessed by my Father; take your inheritance, the kingdom prepared for you since the creation of the world.'"

Matthew 25:34, NIV

The Lord will rescue me from every evil deed and bring me safely into his heavenly kingdom. To him be the glory forever and ever. Amen.

2 Timothy 4:18, ESV

Surely goodness and mercy shall follow me all the days of my life: and I will dwell in the house of the LORD for ever.

Psalm 23:6, KJV

But ye are come unto mount Sion, and unto the city of the living God, the heavenly Jerusalem, and to an innumerable company of angels, To the general assembly and church of the firstborn, which are written in heaven, and to God the Judge of all, and to the spirits of just men made perfect, And to Jesus the mediator of the new covenant, and to the blood of sprinkling, that speaketh better things than that of Abel.

Hebrews 12:22-24, KJV

$\mathcal{H}$ELP

A righteous man may have many troubles, but the
LORD delivers him from them all; he protects all his
bones, not one of them will be broken.

Psalm 34:19-20, NIV

As long as you trust in your own abilities,
there will always be times when you shy
away from a challenge or responsibility. The
result is a feeling of failure or inadequacy.
This usually has a negative effect on your
self-confidence and your ability to handle
a crisis.

You must remember that when God calls
you to do something, He chose you because
He knows that you can fulfil this specific
calling. God does not necessarily call the
ones who are able: He enables those whom
He calls. In Christ your Lord, God will grant
you the ability to fulfil your calling.

Regardless what task you are called to
do, pray about it and dedicate your task to
Christ. Seek the Holy Spirit's help and assis-
tance and follow obediently and willingly
wherever He leads you. You will not fail,
because God Himself will be with you.

HELP IN

HARD TIMES

But the salvation of the righteous is of the LORD: he is their strength in the time of trouble. And the LORD shall help them and deliver them: he shall deliver them from the wicked, and save them, because they trust in him.

Psalm 37:39-40, KJV

Be not far from me; for trouble is near; for there is none to help. But be not thou far from me, O LORD: O my strength, haste thee to help me. Ye that fear the LORD, praise him; all ye the seed of Jacob, glorify him; and fear him, all ye the seed of Israel. For he hath not despised nor abhorred the affliction of the afflicted; neither hath he hid his face from him; but when he cried unto him, he heard.

Psalm 22:11, 19, 23-24, KJV

"These things I have spoken to you, that in Me you may have peace. In the world you will have tribulation; but be of good cheer, I have overcome the world."

John 16:33, NKJV

The LORD is king forever and ever; the nations perish from his land. O LORD, you hear the desire of the afflicted; you will strengthen their heart; you will incline your ear to do justice to the fatherless and the oppressed.

Psalm 10:16-18, ESV

Blessed is he whose help is the God of Jacob, whose hope is in the LORD his God, who made heaven and earth, the sea, and all that is in them, who keeps faith forever; who executes justice for the oppressed, who gives food to the hungry. The LORD sets the prisoners free; the LORD watches over the sojourners; he upholds the widow and the fatherless, but the way of the wicked he brings to ruin.

Psalm 146:5-7, 9, ESV

The LORD is my rock and my fortress and my deliverer; my God, my strength, in whom I will trust; my shield and the horn of my salvation, my stronghold.

Psalm 18:2, NKJV

For the Lord GOD will help me; therefore shall I not be confounded: therefore have I set my face like a flint, and I know that I shall not be ashamed. He is near that justifieth me; who will contend with me? let us stand together: who is mine adversary? let him come near to me. Behold, the Lord GOD will help me; who is he that shall condemn me? lo, they all shall wax old as a garment; the moth shall eat them up.

Isaiah 50:7-9, KJV

Do you not know? Have you not heard? The LORD is the everlasting God, the Creator of the ends of the earth. He will not grow tired or weary, and his understanding no one can fathom. He gives strength to the weary and increases the power of the weak. Even youths grow tired and weary, and young men stumble and fall; but those who hope in the LORD will renew their strength. They will soar on wings like eagles; they will run and not grow weary, they will walk and not be faint.

Isaiah 40:28-31, NIV

$\mathcal{H}$OPE

For to this end we toil and strive, because we have our hope set on the living God, who is the Savior of all people, especially of those who believe.
1 *Timothy 4:10, ESV*

Hope or despair is found in the hearts of people and not in circumstances. Love is the triumph of hope. When things are at their darkest and worst, hope appears in the form of love to light up the dark of night. There is no room in the economy of God for despair, because He has enough love to avert it. Hope is woven into the nature of man so that we may trust in the future.

No man is able to visualize eternity, therefore God granted us hope out of love. What oxygen does for the lungs, hope does for the soul: without it we would die inwardly. When all is hopeless, then hope keeps us going. Hope is the battle of the soul to enable us to hold onto eternity and onto the love of God. If it were not for hope, we would all have had broken hearts. Praise the Lord, for He is good. His love is infinite. He gives us hope out of love.

Hope for

THE HOPELESS

It is written: "No eye has seen, no ear has heard, no mind has conceived what God has prepared for those who love him."

1 Corinthians 2:9, NIV

Why art thou cast down, O my soul? and why art thou disquieted within me? hope thou in God: for I shall yet praise him, who is the health of my countenance, and my God.

Psalm 42:11, KJV

Humble yourselves, therefore, under the mighty hand of God so that at the proper time he may exalt you, casting all your anxieties on him, because he cares for you. Be sober-minded; be watchful. And after you have suffered a little while, the God of all grace, who has called you to his eternal glory in Christ, will himself restore, confirm, strengthen, and establish you.

1 Peter 5:6-10, ESV

I waited patiently for the LORD; and he inclined unto me, and heard my cry. He brought me up also out of an horrible pit, out of the miry clay, and set my feet upon a rock, and established my goings. And he hath put a new song in my mouth, even praise unto our God: many shall see it, and fear, and shall trust in the LORD.

Psalm 40:1-3, KJV

We rejoice in the hope of the glory of God. Not only so, but we also rejoice in our sufferings, because we know that suffering produces perseverance; perseverance, character; and character, hope. And hope does not disappoint us, because God has poured out his love into our hearts by the Holy Spirit, whom he has given us.

Romans 5:2-5, NIV

I wait for the LORD, my soul waits, and in His word I do hope. My soul waits for the LORD more than those who watch for the morning – yes, more than those who watch for the morning. O Israel, hope in the LORD; for with the LORD there is mercy, and with Him is abundant redemption.

Psalm 130:5-7, NKJV

Behold, the eye of the LORD is on those who fear Him, on those who hope in His mercy, to deliver their soul from death, and to keep them alive in famine. Our soul waits for the LORD; He is our help and our shield.

Psalm 33:18-20, NKJV

For we are saved by hope: but hope that is seen is not hope: for what a man seeth, why doth he yet hope for? But if we hope for that we see not, then do we with patience wait for it.

Romans 8:24-25, KJV

Let us hold fast the confession of our hope without wavering, for he who promised is faithful.

Hebrews 10:23, ESV

This I recall to my mind, therefore have I hope. It is of the LORD's mercies that we are not consumed, because his compassions fail not. They are new every morning: great is thy faithfulness. The LORD is my portion, saith my soul; therefore will I hope in him.

Lamentations 3:21-24, KJV

$\mathcal{I}$MPATIENCE

Let us not grow weary while doing good, for in due season we shall reap if we do not lose heart.

Galatians 6:9, NKJV

There are special seasons for the gifts of the Heavenly Father. Many a man asks in April a gift of Divine fruit that will only be ripe in June. Take the case of Paul. Immediately after his conversion he prayed for a mission. He was answered by being sent into the solitudes of Arabia. Was the gratification of his prayer denied, then? No, it was postponed. The mission was coming, but it was coming with the developed years; it was hid in the bosom of the Father till the acceptable time.

My Father, help me to learn that I am heir to possessions which exceed my present holding! They exceed my present *power* to hold – they are waiting for my summer. Do I ever thank Thee for the blessings which Thou postponest? I am afraid not. And, where it is not given, I deem it is refused. Teach me, O Lord, the beauty of Thy delayed answers.

The Word's view

on impatience

A man's wisdom gives him patience; it is to his glory to overlook an offense.

Proverbs 19:11, NIV

Wait on the LORD: be of good courage, and he shall strengthen thine heart: wait, I say, on the LORD.

Psalm 27:14, KJV

Be patient, therefore, brothers, until the coming of the Lord. See how the farmer waits for the precious fruit of the earth, being patient about it, until it receives the early and the late rains. You also, be patient. Establish your hearts, for the coming of the Lord is at hand.

James 5:7-8, ESV

Because you have kept my word about patient endurance, I will keep you from the hour of trial that is coming on the whole world, to try those who dwell on the earth. I am coming soon. Hold fast what you have, so that no one may seize your crown.

Revelation 3:10-11, ESV

We desire that each one of you show the same diligence to the full assurance of hope until the end, that you do not become sluggish, but imitate those who through faith and patience inherit the promises.

Hebrews 6:11-12, NKJV

The Lord is not slow in keeping his promise, as some understand slowness. He is patient with you, not wanting anyone to perish, but everyone to come to repentance.

2 Peter 3:9, NIV

Rest in the LORD, and wait patiently for Him; do not fret because of him who prospers in his way, because of the man who brings wicked schemes to pass. For evildoers shall be cut off; but those who wait on the LORD, they shall inherit the earth.

Psalm 37:7, 9, NKJV

I wait for the LORD, my soul waits, and in his word I put my hope. My soul waits for the LORD more than watchmen wait for the morning, more than watchmen wait for the morning.

Psalm 130:5-6, NIV

THE JOY OF

JUSTIFICATION

All have sinned and fall short of the glory of God, and are justified freely by his grace through the redemption that came by Christ Jesus.

Romans 3:23-24, NIV

God demonstrates His own love toward us, in that while we were still sinners, Christ died for us. Much more then, having now been justified by His blood, we shall be saved from wrath through Him.

Romans 5:8-9, NKJV

God made him who had no sin to be sin for us, so that in him we might become the righteousness of God.

2 Corinthians 5:21, NIV

A man is justified by faith.

Romans 3:28, KJV

Those whom he predestined he also called, and those whom he called he also justified, and those whom he justified he also glorified.

Romans 8:30, ESV

Knowing that a man is not justified by the works of the law, but by the faith of Jesus Christ, even we have believed in Jesus Christ, that we might be justified by the faith of Christ, and not by the works of the law: for by the works of the law shall no flesh be justified.

Galatians 2:16, KJV

He saved us through the washing of rebirth and renewal by the Holy Spirit, whom he poured out on us generously through Jesus Christ our Savior, so that, having been justified by his grace, we might become heirs having the hope of eternal life.

Titus 3:5, 7, NIV

I have fought the good fight, I have finished the race, I have kept the faith. Henceforth there is laid up for me the crown of righteousness, which the Lord, the righteous judge, will award to me on that Day, and not only to me but also to all who have loved his appearing.

2 Timothy 4:7-8, ESV

But let justice run down like water, And righteousness like a mighty stream.

Amos 5:24, NKJV

Through Jesus the forgiveness of sins is proclaimed to you. Through him everyone who believes is justified from everything you could not be justified from by the law of Moses.

Acts 13:38-39, NIV

I will greatly rejoice in the LORD, my soul shall be joyful in my God; for he hath clothed me with the garments of salvation, he hath covered me with the robe of righteousness.

Isaiah 61:10, KJV

For in the gospel a righteousness from God is revealed, a righteousness that is by faith from first to last, just as it is written: "The righteous will live by faith."

Romans 1:17, NIV

Since we have been justified by faith, we have peace with God through our Lord Jesus Christ. Through him we have also obtained access by faith into this grace in which we stand, and we rejoice in hope of the glory of God.

Romans 5:1-2, ESV

*L*ONELINESS

And they that know thy name will put their trust in thee: for thou, LORD, hast not forsaken them that seek thee.

Psalm 9:10, KJV

To have someone to whom you can turn and with whom you can share your life experience is one of God's greatest gifts of grace. It is therefore no wonder that parting with a loved one fills us with sorrow and loneliness. However, you are never alone, because nothing in all of creation can separate us from the love of God in Jesus Christ (see Rom. 8:38-39). The Lord assures us that He will never abandon or forsake us (see Heb. 13:5). These are promises that you can hold on to and draw courage and strength from in all circumstances, especially when tragedy comes into your life and you are at your most vulnerable.

Share all your fears and worries with Him, as well as your loneliness and vulnerability. Christ is not only the Lord of your life, but also your Friend, and remember that He chose you to belong to Him.

Comfort for

the lonely

Where shall I go from your Spirit? Or where shall I flee from your presence? If I ascend to heaven, you are there! If I make my bed in Sheol, you are there! If I take the wings of the morning and dwell in the uttermost parts of the sea, even there your hand shall lead me, and your right hand shall hold me.

Psalm 139:7-10, ESV

Who shall separate us from the love of Christ? shall tribulation, or distress, or persecution, or famine, or nakedness, or peril, or sword? For I am persuaded, that neither death, nor life, nor angels, nor principalities, nor powers, nor things present, nor things to come, nor height, nor depth, nor any other creature, shall be able to separate us from the love of God, which is in Christ Jesus our Lord.

Romans 8:35, 38-39, KJV

Because you are precious in my eyes, and honored, and I love you, I give men in return for you, peoples in exchange for your life. Fear not, for I am with you.

Isaiah 43:4-5, ESV

He Himself has said, "I will never leave you nor forsake you."

Hebrews 13:5, NKJV

"I will not leave you as orphans; I will come to you."

John 14:18, NIV

Then you shall call, and the LORD will answer; you shall cry, and He will say, 'Here I am.'

Isaiah 58:9, NKJV

"I am with you and will keep you wherever you go, and will bring you back to this land; for I will not leave you until I have done what I have spoken to you."

Genesis 28:15, NKJV

"Surely I am with you always, to the very end of the age."

Matthew 28:20, NIV

For David says concerning him, "I saw the Lord always before me, for he is at my right hand that I may not be shaken."

Acts 2:25, ESV

"Indeed the hour is coming, yes, has now come, that you will be scattered, each to his own, and will leave Me alone. And yet I am not alone, because the Father is with Me."

John 16:32, NKJV

"For the mountains may depart and the hills be removed, but my steadfast love shall not depart from you, and my covenant of peace shall not be removed," says the LORD, who has compassion on you.

Isaiah 54:10, ESV

Turn to me and be gracious to me, for I am lonely and afflicted. The troubles of my heart have multiplied; free me from my anguish.

Psalm 25:16-17, NIV

A father to the fatherless, a defender of widows, is God in his holy dwelling. God sets the lonely in families, he leads forth the prisoners with singing; but the rebellious live in a sun-scorched land.

Psalm 68:5-6, NIV

*L*OVE

I pray that you, being rooted and established in love, may have power, together with all the saints, to grasp how wide and long and high and deep is the love of Christ, and to know this love that surpasses knowledge.

Ephesians 3:17-19, NIV

The Spirit of Love, wherever it is, is its own blessing and happiness, because it is the truth and reality of God in the soul, and therefore is the same joy of life and is the same good to itself everywhere and on every occasion. Would you know the blessing of all the blessings? It is the God of love dwelling in your soul and killing every root of bitterness, which is the pain and torment of every earthly, selfish love. For all wants are satisfied, all disorders of every nature are removed, no life is any longer a burden, every day is a day of peace, everything you meet becomes a help to you because everything you see or do is all done in the sweet, gentle element of Love.

THE PROMISE
OF GOD'S LOVE

Beloved, let us love one another, for love is of God; and everyone who loves is born of God and knows God. He who does not love does not know God, for God is love.

1 John 4:7-8, NKJV

"For God so loved the world, that he gave his only Son, that whoever believes in him should not perish but have eternal life."

John 3:16, ESV

So we have come to know and to believe the love that God has for us. God is love, and whoever abides in love abides in God, and God abides in him.

1 John 4:16, ESV

But God, being rich in mercy, because of the great love with which he loved us, even when we were dead in our trespasses, made us alive together with Christ.

Ephesians 2:4-5, ESV

Walk in love, as Christ also has loved us and given Himself for us, an offering and a sacrifice to God for a sweet-smelling aroma.

Ephesians 5:2, NKJV

"A new commandment I give to you, that you love one another; as I have loved you, that you also love one another. By this all will know that you are My disciples, if you have love for one another."

John 13:34-35, NKJV

God demonstrates his own love for us in this: While we were still sinners, Christ died for us.

Romans 5:8, NIV

Let no debt remain outstanding, except the continuing debt to love one another, for he who loves his fellowman has fulfilled the law. The commandments, "Do not commit adultery," "Do not murder," "Do not steal," "Do not covet," and whatever other commandment there may be, are summed up in this one rule: "Love your neighbor as yourself." Love does no harm to its neighbor. Therefore love is the fulfillment of the law.

Romans 13:8-10, NIV

"As the Father hath loved me, so have I loved you: continue ye in my love. If ye keep my commandments, ye shall abide in my love; even as I have kept my Father's commandments, and abide in his love."

John 15:9-10, KJV

Though I speak with the tongues of men and of angels, but have not love, I have become sounding brass or a clanging cymbal. And though I have the gift of prophecy, and understand all mysteries and all knowledge, and though I have all faith, so that I could remove mountains, but have not love, I am nothing. And though I bestow all my goods to feed the poor, and though I give my body to be burned, but have not love, it profits me nothing. Love suffers long and is kind; love does not envy; love does not parade itself, is not puffed up; does not behave rudely, does not seek its own, is not provoked, thinks no evil; does not rejoice in iniquity, but rejoices in the truth; bears all things, believes all things, hopes all things, endures all things. Love never fails.

1 Corinthians 13:1-8, NKJV

MERCY

The LORD is gracious and merciful, slow to anger and abounding in steadfast love. The LORD is good to all, and his mercy is over all that he has made.

Psalm 145:8-9, ESV

Longsuffering and gentleness are marks of a disposition that is Godlike. They are the gentle qualities and fragrant fruit that come only from a full enduement of the Spirit of grace. The godly character of which these graces form a part is strong and discriminating. Longsuffering does not fail to see the fault, but it also appreciates the difficulties, and extenuates the other by a full understanding of the frailty of human nature. Gentleness is not weakness but strength that is held in control and that works with sympathy.

These qualities make one approachable and helpful, and it is to the longsuffering and gentle that bruised and wounded souls turn for help and counsel. They grow in the life that is yielded and trustful; they flourish where faith and obedience to God and His Word are at the root of the spiritual life. Such a disposition forgives for Christ's sake.

GOD'S PROMISE

OF MERCY

"But love ye your enemies, and do good, and lend, hoping for nothing again; and your reward shall be great, and ye shall be the children of the Highest: for he is kind unto the unthankful and to the evil. Be ye therefore merciful, as your Father also is merciful. Judge not, and ye shall not be judged: condemn not, and ye shall not be condemned: forgive, and ye shall be forgiven."

Luke 6:35-37, KJV

For the LORD your God is a merciful God. He will not leave you or destroy you or forget the covenant with your fathers.

Deuteronomy 4:31, ESV

Keep yourselves in the love of God, waiting for the mercy of our Lord Jesus Christ that leads to eternal life.

Jude 1:21, ESV

For I desire mercy and not sacrifice, and the knowledge of God more than burnt offerings.

Hosea 6:6, NKJV

And he said, I will make all my goodness pass before thee, and I will proclaim the name of the LORD before thee; and will be gracious to whom I will be gracious, and will shew mercy on whom I will shew mercy.

Exodus 33:19, KJV

What does the LORD require of you? To act justly and to love mercy and to walk humbly with your God.

Micah 6:8, NIV

But God, who is rich in mercy, for his great love wherewith he loved us, Even when we were dead in sins, hath quickened us together with Christ, (by grace ye are saved;) And hath raised us up together, and made us sit together in heavenly places in Christ Jesus.

Ephesians 2:4-6, KJV

"I am merciful," says the Lord; "I will not remain angry forever. Only acknowledge your iniquity."

Jeremiah 3:12-13, NKJV

Have mercy on me, O God, according to your steadfast love; according to your abundant mercy blot out my transgressions.

Psalm 51:1, ESV

Let us then approach the throne of grace with confidence, so that we may receive mercy and find grace to help us in our time of need.

Hebrews 4:16, NIV

Who is a God like you, pardoning iniquity and passing over transgression for the remnant of his inheritance? He does not retain his anger forever, because he delights in steadfast love.

Micah 7:18, ESV

Remember, O LORD, thy tender mercies and thy lovingkindnesses; for they have been ever of old. Remember not the sins of my youth, nor my transgressions: according to thy mercy remember thou me for thy goodness' sake, O LORD.

Psalm 25:6-7, KJV

Let the wicked forsake his way and the evil man his thoughts. Let him turn to the LORD, and he will have mercy on him, and to our God, for he will freely pardon.

Isaiah 55:7, NIV

OBEDIENCE

*Now therefore, if you will indeed obey my voice
and keep my covenant, you shall be my treasured
possession among all peoples.*
Exodus 19:5, ESV

Effective discipleship requires unconditional
obedience to Christ. This means that your
life should be in harmony with His will and
everything contrary to His will is cast off.

Striving to obey God's will as revealed
to you by the Holy Spirit should be the most
important priority in the life of every Christian. To walk with God; to discern His will
for you through prayer, to know the joy and
peace that come from intimate fellowship
with Him, is the glorious reward of the
committed, obedient disciple.

Obedience to the Lord is not a burdensome duty that must be borne in suffering
silence, or something to be grappled with,
but an indescribable privilege that should
be accepted and carried out with thanksgiving.

The Word's View

ON OBEDIENCE

I have set before you today life and good, death and evil, in that I command you today to love the LORD your God, to walk in His ways, and to keep His commandments, His statutes, and His judgments, that you may live and multiply; and the Lord your God will bless you in the land which you go to possess. But if your heart turns away so that you do not hear, and are drawn away, and worship other gods and serve them, I announce to you today that you shall surely perish.

Deuteronomy 30:15-18, NKJV

Whatever you have learned or received or heard from me, or seen in me – put it into practice. And the God of peace will be with you.

Philippians 4:9, NIV

He stretched out His hand toward His disciples and said, "Here are My mother and My brothers! For whoever does the will of My Father in heaven is My brother and sister and mother."

Matthew 12:49-50, NKJV

Through him and for his name's sake, we received grace and apostleship to call people from among all the Gentiles to the obedience that comes from faith.

Romans 1:5, NIV

To do righteousness and justice is more acceptable to the LORD than sacrifice.

Proverbs 21:3, ESV

This is how we know that we love the children of God: by loving God and carrying out his commands. This is love for God: to obey his commands.

1 John 5:2-3, NIV

"Whoever therefore breaks one of the least of these commandments, and teaches men so, shall be called least in the kingdom of heaven; but whoever does and teaches them, he shall be called great in the kingdom of heaven."

Matthew 5:19, NKJV

Beloved, if our heart does not condemn us, we have confidence before God; and whatever we ask we receive from him, because we keep his commandments and do what pleases him.

1 John 3:21-22, ESV

"Not every one that saith unto me, Lord, Lord, shall enter into the kingdom of heaven; but he that doeth the will of my Father which is in heaven."

Matthew 7:21, KJV

"If you keep my commandments, you will abide in my love, just as I have kept my Father's commandments and abide in his love."

John 15:10, ESV

It is not those who hear the law who are righteous in God's sight, but it is those who obey the law who will be declared righteous.

Romans 2:13, NIV

Submit yourselves, then, to God. Resist the devil, and he will flee from you.

James 4:7, NIV

"Therefore whosoever heareth these sayings of mine, and doeth them, I will liken him unto a wise man, which built his house upon a rock: And the rain descended, and the floods came, and the winds blew, and beat upon that house; and it fell not: for it was founded upon a rock."

Matthew 7:24-25, KJV

$\mathcal{P}$EACE

Blessed are the peacemakers: for they shall be called
the children of God.

Matthew 5:9, KJV

There are many people in this world who are living under a cloud of anxiety, concern and fear. How can one find peace in the midst of such situations?

In difficult circumstances it is especially true that you can do nothing in your own strength to solve your problems. Jesus, our Master, has said that we can do nothing of ourselves, but He also said that with God all things are possible (see Jn. 15:1-8).

In spite of your difficult circumstances and regardless of how unsure the future might seem, your peace of mind will only be secured when you become still before the Lord in prayer. Prayer and meditation, in conjunction with praise and thanksgiving, is the only infallible method to ensure that you will be able to accept and overcome life's challenges. Do not rob yourself of this opportunity to find peace!

THE PROMISE
OF PEACE

Let the peace of Christ rule in your hearts, since as members of one body you were called to peace.

Colossians 3:15, NIV

Do not be anxious about anything, but in everything by prayer and supplication with thanksgiving let your requests be made known to God. And the peace of God, which surpasses all understanding, will guard your hearts and your minds in Christ Jesus.

Philippians 4:6-7, ESV

"Whoever desires to love life and see good days, let him keep his tongue from evil and his lips from speaking deceit; let him seek peace and pursue it."

1 Peter 3:10-11, ESV

"Peace I leave with you, my peace I give unto you: not as the world giveth, give I unto you. Let not your heart be troubled, neither let it be afraid."

John 14:27, KJV

Thou wilt keep him in perfect peace, whose mind is stayed on thee: because he trusteth in thee.

Isaiah 26:3, KJV

Now may the Lord of peace himself give you peace at all times and in every way. The Lord be with all of you.

2 Thessalonians 3:16, NIV

Make every effort to keep the unity of the Spirit through the bond of peace.

Ephesians 4:3, NIV

Better a dry crust with peace and quiet than a house full of feasting, with strife.

Proverbs 17:1, NIV

You will keep him in perfect peace, whose mind is stayed on You, because he trusts in You.

Isaiah 26:3, NKJV

And he came and preached peace to you who were far off and peace to those who were near.

Ephesians 2:17, ESV

I will both lay me down in peace, and sleep:
for thou, LORD, only makest me dwell in
safety.

Psalm 4:8, KJV

And the fruit of righteousness is sown in
peace of them that make peace.

James 3:18, KJV

For God is not the author of confusion but
of peace.

1 Corinthians 14:33, NKJV

For he himself is our peace, who has made
the two one and has destroyed the barrier,
the dividing wall of hostility, by abolishing
in his flesh the law with its commandments
and regulations. His purpose was to create
in himself one new man out of the two,
thus making peace, and in this one body
to reconcile both of them to God through
the cross, by which he put to death their
hostility. He came and preached peace to
you who were far away and peace to those
who were near. For through him we both
have access to the Father by one Spirit.

Ephesians 2:14-18, NIV

$\mathscr{P}$ERSEVERANCE

For you have need of endurance, so that when you have done the will of God you may receive what is promised.

Hebrews 10:36, ESV

There are few things as sad as the failure to see results from your efforts. If after much effort and perseverance, you still see no signs of success, you become discouraged. We will never know how many worthwhile tasks were never completed because the people involved in them became discouraged.

A study of the spiritual giants in the Bible will reveal how they persevered against enormous odds as they did the work of God. Regardless of setback, ridicule, resistance in the face of unbelievable suffering, they persevered with determination, until the glory of God's purpose was revealed.

At times things will become very difficult and you will be tempted to believe that your efforts are useless. Let faith triumph over your feelings and rest assured that, in God's perfect timing, your efforts will bear fruit to the glory of His Name.

Promises for those

who persevere

He will keep you strong to the end, so that you will be blameless on the day of our Lord Jesus Christ.

1 Corinthians 1:8, NKJV

We rejoice in the hope of the glory of God. Not only so, but we also rejoice in our sufferings, because we know that suffering produces perseverance; perseverance, character; and character, hope.

Romans 5:2-4, NIV

Consider it pure joy, my brothers, whenever you face trials of many kinds, because you know that the testing of your faith develops perseverance. Perseverance must finish its work so that you may be mature and complete, not lacking anything.

James 1:2-4, NIV

Blessed is the man who perseveres under trial, because when he has stood the test, he will receive the crown of life that God has promised to those who love him.

James 1:12, NIV

Indeed we count them blessed who endure. You have heard of the perseverance of Job and seen the end intended by the Lord – that the Lord is very compassionate and merciful.

James 5:11, NKJV

Therefore, since we are surrounded by so great a cloud of witnesses, let us also lay aside every weight, and sin which clings so closely, and let us run with endurance the race that is set before us, looking to Jesus, the founder and perfecter of our faith, who for the joy that was set before him endured the cross, despising the shame, and is seated at the right hand of the throne of God. Consider him who endured from sinners such hostility against himself, so that you may not grow weary or fainthearted.

Hebrews 12:1-3, ESV

And let us not grow weary of doing good, for in due season we will reap, if we do not give up.

Galatians 6:9, ESV

I can do all things through Christ who strengthens me.

Philippians 4:13, NKJV

Be strong in the Lord and in the power of His might. Put on the whole armor of God, that you may be able to stand against the wiles of the devil.

Ephesians 6:10-11, NKJV

To those who by persistence in doing good seek glory, honor and immortality, he will give eternal life.

Romans 2:7, NIV

Here is the patience of the saints: here are they that keep the commandments of God, and the faith of Jesus.

Revelation 14:12, KJV

I know your deeds, your hard work and your perseverance. I know that you cannot tolerate wicked men, that you have tested those who claim to be apostles but are not, and have found them false. You have persevered and have endured hardships for my name, and have not grown weary.

Revelation 2:2-3, NIV

POVERTY

For You have been a strength to the poor, a strength to the needy in his distress, a refuge from the storm, a shade from the heat.

Isaiah 25:4, NKJV

Many people are unaware of the immeasurable generosity of God. Their own needs and dire poverty blind them and separate them from the One who could ease their suffering and transform their poverty into luxury, if only they would obey Him.

Scripture reveals to us the joyful fact that God is much more willing to give than we are to receive. If we would only pray and believe sincerely and in faith, we could receive that which we pray for. Many disciples want to believe unconditionally and yet there are few who want to utilize the key which God makes available to unlock His abundance.

If you bring a request to your heavenly Father, make sure you don't harbor doubt that He won't comply with your request. God hears your prayers and will meet your every need from His treasure house – according to His glorious grace.

Promises in
Times of Poverty

The LORD maketh poor, and maketh rich: he bringeth low, and lifteth up. He raiseth up the poor out of the dust, and lifteth up the beggar from the dunghill, to set them among princes, and to make them inherit the throne of glory: for the pillars of the earth are the LORD's, and he hath set the world upon them.

1 Samuel 2:7-8, KJV

Has not God chosen those who are poor in the world to be rich in faith and heirs of the kingdom, which he has promised to those who love him?

James 2:5, ESV

Open thy mouth, judge righteously, and plead the cause of the poor and needy.

Proverbs 31:9, KJV

"The poor and needy seek water, but there is none, their tongues fail for thirst. I, the LORD, will hear them; I, the God of Israel, will not forsake them."

Isaiah 41:17, NKJV

The king that faithfully judgeth the poor, his throne shall be established for ever.

Proverbs 29:14, KJV

If there is a poor man among your brothers in any of the towns of the land that the LORD your God is giving you, do not be hardhearted or tightfisted toward your poor brother. Rather be openhanded and freely lend him whatever he needs. Give generously to him and do so without a grudging heart; then because of this the LORD your God will bless you in all your work and in everything you put your hand to. There will always be poor people in the land. Therefore I command you to be openhanded toward your brothers and toward the poor and needy in your land.

Deuteronomy 15:7-8, 10-11, NIV

If ye fulfil the royal law according to the scripture, Thou shalt love thy neighbour as thyself, ye do well.

James 2:8, KJV

All my bones shall say, "O LORD, who is like you, delivering the poor from him who is too strong for him, the poor and needy from him who robs him?"

Psalm 35:10, ESV

And oppress not the widow, nor the fatherless, the stranger, nor the poor; and let none of you imagine evil against his brother in your heart.

Zechariah 7:10, KJV

"'Lord, when did we see You hungry and feed You, or thirsty and give You drink? When did we see You a stranger and take You in, or naked and clothe You? Or when did we see You sick, or in prison, and come to You?' And the King will answer and say to them, 'Assuredly, I say to you, inasmuch as you did it to one of the least of these My brethren, you did it to Me.'"

Matthew 25:37-40, NKJV

Religion that is pure and undefiled before God and the Father is this: to visit orphans and widows in their affliction, and to keep oneself unstained from the world.

James 1:27, ESV

You evildoers frustrate the plans of the poor, but the LORD is their refuge.

Psalm 14:6, KJV

$\mathscr{P}$RAISE

Praise the LORD, for the LORD is good; sing to his name,
for it is pleasant! Blessed be the LORD from Zion, he
who dwells in Jerusalem! Praise the LORD!
Psalm 135:3, 21, ESV

The Lord is worthy; all His attributes unite to call forth our praise. The Father is to be praised for His eternal love and wisdom, the Son for His redeeming work, and the Spirit for His saving and sanctifying grace. All God's ways with man call us to praise and magnify Him.

Praise is a sacrifice that we offer to God Himself. There is little that we can give to God, but praise from a redeemed heart is precious to Him. A heart to praise our God and full of love divine is the first requisite for helping to turn other sinners to the saving grace of God. If only we praised God more, and more spontaneously, then the world around, unsatisfied and grumbling, would surely take note that we have a Friend who means much to us.

Precious

PRAISE

Though the fig tree does not bud and there are no grapes on the vines, though the olive crop fails and the fields produce no food, though there are no sheep in the pen and no cattle in the stalls, yet I will rejoice in the LORD, I will be joyful in God my Savior.

Habakkuk 3:17-18, NIV

O come, let us worship and bow down: let us kneel before the LORD our maker. For he is our God; and we are the people of his pasture, and the sheep of his hand.

Psalm 95:6-7, KJV

Great is the LORD, and greatly to be praised, and his greatness is unsearchable.

Psalm 145:3, ESV

I will praise You, O LORD, among the peoples; I will sing to You among the nations. For Your mercy reaches unto the heavens, and Your truth unto the clouds. Be exalted, O God, above the heavens; let Your glory be above all the earth.

Psalm 57:9-11, NKJV

Sing unto the LORD, praise ye the LORD: for he hath delivered the soul of the poor from the hand of evildoers.

Jeremiah 20:13, KJV

You are a chosen generation, a royal priesthood, a holy nation, His own special people, that you may proclaim the praises of Him who called you out of darkness into His marvelous light.

1 Peter 2:9, NKJV

Praise ye the LORD. Praise God in his sanctuary: praise him in the firmament of his power. Praise him for his mighty acts: praise him according to his excellent greatness. Praise him with the sound of the trumpet: praise him with the psaltery and harp. Praise him with the timbrel and dance: praise him with stringed instruments and organs. Praise him upon the loud cymbals: praise him upon the high sounding cymbals. Let every thing that hath breath praise the LORD.

Psalm 150:1-6, KJV

Sing unto the LORD, O ye saints of his, and give thanks at the remembrance of his holiness.

Psalm 30:4, KJV

Bless the LORD, O my soul, and all that is within me, bless his holy name! Bless the LORD, O my soul, and forget not all his benefits.

Psalm 103:1-2, ESV

O LORD, thou art my God; I will exalt thee, I will praise thy name; for thou hast done wonderful things; thy counsels of old are faithfulness and truth.

Isaiah 25:1, KJV

Praise the LORD. I will extol the LORD with all my heart in the council of the upright and in the assembly. Great are the works of the LORD; they are pondered by all who delight in them. Glorious and majestic are his deeds, and his righteousness endures forever.

Psalm 111:1-3, NIV

Sing, O heavens, for the LORD has done it! Shout, you lower parts of the earth; break forth into singing, you mountains, O forest, and every tree in it! For the LORD has redeemed Jacob, and glorified Himself in Israel.

Isaiah 44:23-24, NKJV

$\mathscr{P}$RAYER

*Hear my prayer, O L*ORD*; listen to my cry for mercy.*
In the day of my trouble I will call to you, for you
will answer me.

Psalm 86:6-7, NIV

Prayer power is not only the most direct, but also the most effective force that can be brought to bear upon the many difficult problems that exist in the Lord's work. Prayer is not only more effective than other methods of carrying forward the work of the Lord, but it has also the further great advantage of being free from human schemes and carnal manipulations.

He who waits upon God, moves on in quiet confidence and needs neither the blare of trumpets nor press agents' methods to announce his success, but in godly fear, leaves until the day of Christ's return the record of achievement. The whole tendency in the life of prayer is to bring us to the place of crucifixion, and to school us in the great principles of righteousness, justice, and love.

PROMISES FOR

THOSE WHO PRAY

Evening and morning and at noon I utter my complaint and he hears my voice.

Psalm 55:17, ESV

"Lord, teach us to pray, as John taught his disciples." And he said to them, "When you pray, say: 'Father, hallowed be your name. Your kingdom come. Give us each day our daily bread, and forgive us our sins, for we ourselves forgive everyone who is indebted to us. And lead us not into temptation.'"

Luke 11:1-4, ESV

Then you shall call, and the LORD will answer; You shall cry, and He will say, "Here I am."

Isaiah 58:9, NKJV

Hear me when I call, O God of my righteousness: thou hast enlarged me when I was in distress; have mercy upon me, and hear my prayer. Know that the LORD hath set apart him that is godly for himself: the LORD will hear when I call unto him.

Psalm 4:1, 3, KJV

Many are they who say of me, "There is no help for him in God." But You, O LORD, are a shield for me, my glory and the One who lifts up my head. I cried to the LORD with my voice, and He heard me from His holy hill.

Psalm 3:2-4, NKJV

I sought the LORD, and He heard me, and delivered me from all my fears.

Psalm 34:4, NKJV

Hear my cry for mercy as I call to you for help, as I lift up my hands toward your Most Holy Place. Praise be to the LORD, for he has heard my cry for mercy. The LORD is my strength and my shield; my heart trusts in him, and I am helped. My heart leaps for joy and I will give thanks to him in song.

Psalm 28:2, 6-7, NIV

Let us then with confidence draw near to the throne of grace, that we may receive mercy and find grace to help in time of need.

Hebrews 4:16, ESV

Before they call I will answer; while they are still speaking I will hear.

Isaiah 65:24, NIV

I pray that out of his glorious riches he may strengthen you with power through his Spirit in your inner being, so that Christ may dwell in your hearts through faith.

Ephesians 3:16-17, NIV

Whatever you do in word or deed, do all in the name of the Lord Jesus, giving thanks to God the Father through Him.

Colossians 3:17, NIV

"Whatever you ask in My name, that I will do, that the Father may be glorified in the Son. If you ask anything in My name, I will do it."

John 14:13-14, NKJV

But from there you will seek the LORD your God and you will find him, if you search after him with all your heart and with all your soul.

Deuteronomy 4:29, ESV

"All things, whatsoever ye shall ask in prayer, believing, ye shall receive."

Matthew 21:22, KJV

PROTECTION

The name of the LORD is a strong tower; the righteous run to it and are safe.

Proverbs 18:10, NKJV

All people need a shelter at some time. It may be the security of home, or a shelter against a storm. In times of war, shelter is sought against falling bombs. Our spiritual and intellectual faculties are often attacked by the storms of life. In order to seek shelter against these and to prevent devastating emotional consequences, we need a haven in life that will be constant and safe and where we can shelter in complete faith.

Regardless of what may happen to you, place your trust and faith in God at all times. Even when it seems as though everything is lost and your world collapses around you like a stack of cards, entrust yourself to the love of Jesus Christ. God has promised never to fail you nor forsake you. With this certainty in your heart, you can face the future with confidence. Regardless of how dark the road ahead may seem, Christ, with His love, is your shelter and safe haven.

Promises

of protection

"Because he holds fast to me in love, I will deliver him; I will protect him, because he knows my name. When he calls to me, I will answer him; I will be with him in trouble; I will rescue him and honor him. With long life I will satisfy him and show him my salvation."

Psalm 91:14-16, ESV

"Holy Father, protect them by the power of your name – the name you gave me – so that they may be one as we are one."

John 17:11, NIV

The eternal God is your refuge, and underneath are the everlasting arms; He will thrust out the enemy from before you, and will say, 'Destroy!'

Deuteronomy 33:27, NKJV

The LORD is my light and my salvation; whom shall I fear? the LORD is the strength of my life; of whom shall I be afraid?

Psalm 27:1, KJV

The Lord is faithful, who will establish you
and guard you from the evil one.

2 Thessalonians 3:3, NKJV

Those who trust in the LORD are like Mount
Zion, which cannot be moved, but abides
forever. As the mountains surround Jerusalem, so the Lord surrounds His people from
this time forth and forever.

Psalm 125:1-2, NKJV

The LORD hear thee in the day of trouble;
the name of the God of Jacob defend thee;
Send thee help from the sanctuary, and
strengthen thee out of Zion.

Psalm 20:1-2, KJV

I will both lay me down in peace, and sleep:
for thou, LORD, only makest me dwell in
safety.

Psalm 4:8, KJV

The LORD will keep you from all evil; he
will keep your life. The LORD will keep your
going out and your coming in from this time
forth and forevermore.

Psalm 121:7-8, ESV

For he will command his angels concerning you to guard you in all your ways; they will lift you up in their hands, so that you will not strike your foot against a stone.

Psalm 91:11-12, NIV

When you pass through the waters, I will be with you; and through the rivers, they shall not overwhelm you; when you walk through fire you shall not be burned, and the flame shall not consume you.

Isaiah 43:2, ESV

One man of you shall chase a thousand: for the LORD your God, he it is that fighteth for you, as he hath promised you.

Joshua 23:10, KJV

Keep me, O LORD, from the hands of the wicked; protect me from men of violence who plan to trip my feet.

Psalm 140:4, NIV

$\mathcal{S}$ALVATION

"Salvation is found in no one else, for there is no other name under heaven given to men by which we must be saved."

Acts 4:12, NIV

Why did Jesus have to die on a cursed tree?

- Because the justice of God demanded it. Man, created in the image of God, was reduced to sin and the penalty for his trespass was his life: the wages of sin is death. Here God's holiness and righteousness are seen.

- The love of God required a sacrifice of His Son: To take our sins upon Himself and to pay for them, the Man of Sorrows had to suffer hammer-blows and nail scars in His body.

What is your answer to the "Why?" of Golgotha? He did it to redeem us. Golgotha draws our attention to the ghastliness of sin so that we can flee from it forever. Golgotha teaches us that God's love is unfathomable so that we can seek shelter with Him and, in doing so, gain eternal life.

Assurance of

salvation

For we ourselves were once foolish, disobedient, led astray, slaves to various passions and pleasures, passing our days in malice and envy, hated by others and hating one another. But when the goodness and loving kindness of God our Savior appeared, he saved us, not because of works done by us in righteousness, but according to his own mercy, by the washing of regeneration and renewal of the Holy Spirit, whom he poured out on us richly through Jesus Christ our Savior, so that being justified by his grace we might become heirs according to the hope of eternal life.

Titus 3:3-7, ESV

By grace you have been saved through faith, and that not of yourselves; it is the gift of God, not of works.

Ephesians 2:8-9, NKJV

Christ was sacrificed once to take away the sins of many people; and he will appear a second time, not to bear sin, but to bring salvation to those who are waiting for him.

Hebrews 9:28, NIV

"For God so loved the world that He gave His only begotten Son, that whoever believes in Him should not perish but have everlasting life. For God did not send His Son into the world to condemn the world, but that the world through Him might be saved."

John 3:16-17, NKJV

"She will bear a son, and you shall call his name Jesus, for he will save his people from their sins."

Matthew 1:21, ESV

But now thus says the LORD, he who created you, O Jacob, he who formed you, O Israel: "Fear not, for I have redeemed you; I have called you by name, you are mine."

Isaiah 43:1, ESV

But now being made free from sin, and become servants to God, ye have your fruit unto holiness, and the end everlasting life.

Romans 6:22, KJV

He has delivered us from the domain of darkness and transferred us to the kingdom of his beloved Son, in whom we have redemption, the forgiveness of sins.

Colossians 1:13-14, ESV

God hath given to us eternal life, and this life is in his Son. He that hath the Son hath life.

1 John 5:11, KJV

When you were dead in your sins and in the uncircumcision of your sinful nature, God made you alive with Christ. He forgave us all our sins.

Colossians 2:13, NIV

If you confess with your mouth the Lord Jesus and believe in your heart that God has raised Him from the dead, you will be saved. For with the heart one believes unto righteousness, and with the mouth confession is made unto salvation.

Romans 10:9-10, NKJV

But God, being rich in mercy, because of the great love with which he loved us, even when we were dead in our trespasses, made us alive together with Christ – by grace you have been saved.

Ephesians 2:4-5, ESV

For whosoever shall call upon the name of the Lord shall be saved.

Romans 10:13, KJV

$\mathscr{S}$ICKNESS

For he maketh sore, and bindeth up: he woundeth,
and his hands make whole.

Job 5:18, KJV

Let us not have any doubt about this: the risen Lord still performs miraculous healings. However, we do not have an answer to the mystery of why some people are healed and others not. When someone suffers from physical ailments, healing is very important to that person – yet, healing of the spirit is equally (if not more) important. Healing of the spirit should be preferred to physical healing, as it has been well-documented that an ailing spirit can cause physical harm. When your spirit is well, you will have a good attitude toward life and the Holy Spirit will be able to flow through you unimpeded and bring healing.

You must rid yourself of everything that separates you from God. He has made forgiveness available through the love-sacrifice of Jesus Christ. He promises His life-giving Spirit to all who acknowledge His authority.

COMFORT

IN SICKNESS

Praise the LORD, O my soul, and forget not
all his benefits – who forgives all your sins
and heals all your diseases.

Psalm 103:2-3, NIV

Is anyone among you sick? Let him call for
the elders of the church, and let them pray
over him, anointing him with oil in the name
of the Lord. And the prayer of faith will save
the sick, and the Lord will raise him up.

James 5:14-15, NKJV

Be not wise in thine own eyes: fear the LORD,
and depart from evil. It shall be health to
thy navel, and marrow to thy bones.

Proverbs 3:7-8, KJV

I pray that you may enjoy good health and
that all may go well with you, even as your
soul is getting along well.

3 John 2, NIV

Heal me, O LORD, and I shall be healed;
save me, and I shall be saved.

Jeremiah 17:14, ESV

Therefore confess your sins to each other and pray for each other so that you may be healed. The prayer of a righteous man is powerful and effective.

James 5:16, NIV

"Heal the sick, raise the dead, cleanse those who have leprosy, drive out demons. Freely you have received, freely give."

Matthew 10:8, NIV

I pleaded with the Lord three times that it might depart from me. And He said to me, "My grace is sufficient for you, for My strength is made perfect in weakness." Therefore most gladly I will rather boast in my infirmities, that the power of Christ may rest upon me. Therefore I take pleasure in infirmities, in reproaches, in needs, in persecutions, in distresses, for Christ's sake. For when I am weak, then I am strong.

2 Corinthians 12:8-10, NKJV

Even though I walk through the valley of the shadow of death, I will fear no evil, for you are with me; your rod and your staff, they comfort me.

Psalm 23:4, ESV

Have mercy on me, O LORD, for I am weak;
O LORD, heal me, for my bones are troubled.
My soul also is greatly troubled.

Psalm 6:2-3, NKJV

The spirit of a man will sustain him in sickness,
but who can bear a broken spirit?

Proverbs 18:14, NKJV

Blessed is he that considereth the poor: the
LORD will deliver him in time of trouble.
The LORD will strengthen him upon the bed
of languishing: thou wilt make all his bed
in his sickness. I said, LORD, be merciful
unto me: heal my soul; for I have sinned
against thee.

Psalm 41:1, 3-4, KJV

Jesus went about all Galilee, teaching in their
synagogues, and preaching the gospel of the
kingdom, and healing all manner of sickness
and all manner of disease among the people.
And his fame went throughout all Syria: and
they brought unto him all sick people that
were taken with divers diseases and torments,
and those which were possessed with devils,
and those which were lunatick, and those
that had the palsy; and he healed them.

Matthew 4:23-24, KJV

Sin

I have blotted out your transgressions like a cloud and your sins like mist; return to me, for I have redeemed you.

Isaiah 44:22, ESV

The greatest of all human griefs is that which manifests through our sins. Grieving about sins includes many things: anxiety about our betrayal of the living God; our shallowness, disobedience and unwillingness to serve Him; our lack of holiness; our refusal to subject ourselves to His holy will; our devotedness to our worldly possessions, and many more.

However, Christ is the Comforter for all who have learned through grace to grieve about their sins and who steadfastly know that, through repentance and remission of sins, they belong to Him. God showed Moses a piece of wood which made the bitter water of Marah sweet. That piece of wood is to us a symbol of the cross: through the bitter cursed tree the source of our sin and sorrow is healed. On this tree He carried *our* sins in His body. On this tree He fully becomes our Comforter, Savior and Redeemer.

The Word's View
ON SIN

Repent ye therefore, and be converted, that your sins may be blotted out, when the times of refreshing shall come from the presence of the Lord.

Acts 3:19, KJV

Who can discern his errors? Forgive my hidden faults. Keep your servant also from willful sins; may they not rule over me. Then will I be blameless.

Psalm 19:12-13, NIV

"For God so loved the world that He gave His only begotten Son, that whoever believes in Him should not perish but have everlasting life. For God did not send His Son into the world to condemn the world, but that the world through Him might be saved."

John 3:16-17, NKJV

For all have sinned, and come short of the glory of God; Being justified freely by his grace through the redemption that is in Christ Jesus.

Romans 3:23-24, KJV

The LORD is merciful and gracious, slow to anger, and abounding in mercy. He will not always strive with us, nor will He keep His anger forever. He has not dealt with us according to our sins, nor punished us according to our iniquities. For as the heavens are high above the earth, so great is His mercy toward those who fear Him; as far as the east is from the west, so far has He removed our transgressions from us.

Psalm 103:8-12, NKJV

For the wages of sin is death; but the gift of God is eternal life through Jesus Christ our Lord.

Romans 6:23, KJV

Blessed is he whose transgression is forgiven, whose sin is covered. I acknowledged my sin unto thee, and mine iniquity have I not hid. I said, I will confess my transgressions unto the LORD; and thou forgavest the iniquity of my sin.

Psalm 32:1, 5, KJV

In this is love, not that we loved God, but that He loved us and sent His Son to be the propitiation for our sins.

1 John 4:10, NKJV

And you, who were dead in your trespasses and the uncircumcision of your flesh, God made alive together with him, having forgiven us all our trespasses, by canceling the record of debt that stood against us with its legal demands. This he set aside, nailing it to the cross.

Colossians 2:13-14, ESV

In him we have redemption through his blood, the forgiveness of sins, in accordance with the riches of God's grace that he lavished on us with all wisdom and understanding.

Ephesians 1:7-8, NIV

Wash me thoroughly from my iniquity, and cleanse me from my sin! Hide your face from my sins, and blot out all my iniquities. Create in me a clean heart, O God, and renew a right spirit within me. Restore to me the joy of your salvation, and uphold me with a willing spirit.

Psalm 51:2, 9-10, 12, ESV

STRESS

I can do all things through Christ which strengtheneth me.

Philippians 4:13, KJV

Across the world people are put under tremendous pressure. Demands continue to increase, and more and more is expected from us. Everywhere people are looking for release from the unbearable stress under which they live each day.

There are, of course, man-made tranquilizers that are used in incredible quantities. For many, these lead to addiction. There are many dangers and side-effects in all man-made solutions, and even though they bring some temporary relief to many, ultimately there is only one way to ensure the peace and rest for which we long. *"My soul finds rest in God alone; my salvation comes from him"* (Ps. 62:1, NIV). Knowing Him and being silent in His presence bring true peace. He invites all those who are tired and over-burdened to take His gentle yoke and He will give them the peace of God that passes all understanding.

STRENGTH IN TIMES

OF STRESS

"Come to me, all you who are weary and burdened, and I will give you rest. Take my yoke upon you and learn from me, for I am gentle and humble in heart, and you will find rest for your souls. For my yoke is easy and my burden is light."

Matthew 11:28-30, NIV

For you are my lamp, O LORD, and my God lightens my darkness. For by you I can run against a troop, and by my God I can leap over a wall. This God – his way is perfect; the word of the LORD proves true; he is a shield for all those who take refuge in him. For who is God, but the LORD? And who is a rock, except our God?

2 Samuel 22:29-32, ESV

The Spirit also helps in our weaknesses. For we do not know what we should pray for as we ought, but the Spirit Himself makes intercession for us with groanings which cannot be uttered.

Romans 8:26, NKJV

Rejoice in the Lord always. I will say it again: Rejoice! Let your gentleness be evident to all. The Lord is near. Do not be anxious about anything, but in everything, by prayer and petition, with thanksgiving, present your requests to God. And the peace of God, will guard your hearts and your minds in Christ Jesus.

Philippians 4:4-7, NIV

Unless the LORD had been my help, my soul had almost dwelt in silence. When I said, My foot slippeth; thy mercy, O LORD, held me up. In the multitude of my thoughts within me thy comforts delight my soul.

Psalm 94:17-19, KJV

"Have I not commanded you? Be strong and courageous. Do not be frightened, and do not be dismayed, for the LORD your God is with you wherever you go."

Joshua 1:9, ESV

Humble yourselves, therefore, under God's mighty hand, that he may lift you up in due time. Cast all your anxiety on him because he cares for you.

1 Peter 5:6-7, NIV

For he will command his angels concerning you to guard you in all your ways. On their hands they will bear you up, lest you strike your foot against a stone. "Because he holds fast to me in love, I will deliver him; I will protect him, because he knows my name. When he calls to me, I will answer him; I will be with him in trouble; I will rescue him and honor him."

Psalm 91:11-12, 14-15, ESV

Blessed is the man who remains steadfast under trial, for when he has stood the test he will receive the crown of life, which God has promised to those who love him.

James 1:12, ESV

"Peace I leave with you; my peace I give you. I do not give to you as the world gives. Do not let your hearts be troubled and do not be afraid."

John 14:27, NIV

The LORD also will be a refuge for the oppressed, a refuge in times of trouble.

Psalm 9:9, KJV

ᴛᴇᴍᴩᴛᴀᴛɪᴏɴ

For in that He Himself has suffered, being tempted,
He is able to aid those who are tempted.

Hebrews 2:18, NKJV

Most Christians experience problems living
in obedience to the commands of the Master.
Some go through barren patches and struggle
with the temptation to compromise with
the sinful world. Many simply give up while
their faith weakens.

Don't forget that Jesus was exposed to
immense temptations. There were moments,
like shortly before His capture and crucifixion, when a compromise of His principles
would have been greatly advantageous to His
human wellbeing. If He had given in, He
would have been spared the horror of the
cross, but He would have robbed Himself
of the glory of the resurrection, and the
world of salvation.

Just as Jesus drew His strength from the
Spirit of God, He proffers His Holy Spirit
to you to enable you to triumph over temptation and to live the way in which He wants
you to live.

THE WORD'S VIEW

ON TEMPTATION

"Enter by the narrow gate; for wide is the gate and broad is the way that leads to destruction, and there are many who go in by it. Because narrow is the gate and difficult is the way which leads to life, and there are few who find it."

Matthew 7:13-14, NKJV

Put on the full armor of God so that you can take your stand against the devil's schemes. For our struggle is not against flesh and blood, but against the rulers, against the authorities, against the powers of this dark world and against the spiritual forces of evil in the heavenly realms. Therefore put on the full armor of God, so that when the day of evil comes, you may be able to stand your ground.

Ephesians 6:11-13, NIV

The Lord knoweth how to deliver the godly out of temptations, and to reserve the unjust unto the day of judgment to be punished.

2 Peter 2:9, KJV

Let no one say when he is tempted, "I am tempted by God"; for God cannot be tempted by evil, nor does He Himself tempt anyone. But each one is tempted when he is drawn away by his own desires and enticed.

James 1:13-14, NKJV

"Watch and pray, that ye enter not into temptation: the spirit indeed is willing, but the flesh is weak."

Matthew 26:41, KJV

No temptation has overtaken you except such as is common to man; but God is faithful, who will not allow you to be tempted beyond what you are able, but with the temptation will also make the way of escape, that you may be able to bear it.

1 Corinthians 10:13, NKJV

Be sober, be vigilant; because your adversary the devil, as a roaring lion, walketh about, seeking whom he may devour.

1 Peter 5:8, KJV

"Lead us not into temptation, but deliver us from the evil one."

Matthew 6:13, NIV

For we do not have a high priest who is unable to sympathize with our weaknesses, but one who in every respect has been tempted as we are, yet without sin. Let us then with confidence draw near to the throne of grace, that we may receive mercy and find grace to help in time of need.

Hebrews 4:15-16, NKJV

Then Jesus was led by the Spirit into the desert to be tempted by the devil. After fasting forty days and forty nights, he was hungry. The tempter came to him and said, "If you are the Son of God, tell these stones to become bread." Jesus answered, "It is written: 'Man does not live on bread alone, but on every word that comes from the mouth of God.'"

Matthew 4:1-4, NIV

Ye are of God, little children, and have overcome them: because greater is he that is in you, than he that is in the world.

1 John 4:4, KJV

ᴛᴏᴍᴏʀʀᴏᴡ

"Therefore do not be anxious about tomorrow, for tomorrow will be anxious for itself. Sufficient for the day is its own trouble."

Matthew 6:34, ESV

All of us at some time or another make plans for the future. In some cases these plans do not materialize – they remain dreams. However, when one plans diligently, dreams are often fulfilled and ambitions realized.

People who leave their future in the hand of "Fate" or "Lady Luck" will find their future clouded with uncertainty. Fate has no part in the life of a Christian. God is always in control! There is only one way that you can be confident about your future: commit your whole life to God. In His perfect time He will lead you into the future that He has planned for you. He has a wonderful blueprint for your life!

Go into the future with your hand in His. Then you will act with confidence and have the peace of mind that comes from knowing that you are living according to God's master plan for your life.

Hope for
Tomorrow

Come now, you who say, "Today or tomorrow we will go into such and such a town and spend a year there and trade and make a profit" – yet you do not know what tomorrow will bring. What is your life? For you are a mist that appears for a little time and then vanishes. Instead you ought to say, "If the Lord wills, we will live and do this or that."

James 4:13-15, ESV

Blessed is the man who trusts in the LORD, whose confidence is in him. He will be like a tree planted by the water that sends out its roots by the stream. It does not fear when heat comes; its leaves are always green. It has no worries in a year of drought and never fails to bear fruit.

Jeremiah 17:7-8, NIV

The LORD is my rock, and my fortress, and my deliverer; my God, my strength, in whom I will trust; my buckler, and the horn of my salvation, and my high tower.

Psalm 18:2, KJV

Fear thou not; for I am with thee: be not dismayed; for I am thy God: I will strengthen thee; yea, I will help thee; yea, I will uphold thee with the right hand of my righteousness. For I the LORD thy God will hold thy right hand, saying unto thee, Fear not; I will help thee.

Isaiah 41:10, 13, KJV

As a father pities his children, so the LORD pities those who fear Him. For He knows our frame; He remembers that we are dust. As for man, his days are like grass; as a flower of the field, so he flourishes. For the wind passes over it, and it is gone, and its place remembers it no more. But the mercy of the LORD is from everlasting to everlasting on those who fear Him, and His righteousness to children's children, to such as keep His covenant, and to those who remember His commandments to do them.

Psalm 103:13-18, NKJV

This one thing I do, forgetting those things which are behind, and reaching forth unto those things which are before, I press toward the mark for the prize of the high calling of God in Christ Jesus.

Philippians 3:13-14, KJV

For I know the thoughts that I think toward you, says the LORD, thoughts of peace and not of evil, to give you a future and a hope.

Jeremiah 29:11, NKJV

A man's heart deviseth his way: but the LORD directeth his steps.

Proverbs 16:9, KJV

And your ears shall hear a word behind you, saying, "This is the way, walk in it," when you turn to the right or when you turn to the left.

Isaiah 30:21, ESV

He who began a good work in you will carry it on to completion until the day of Christ Jesus.

Philippians 1:6, NIV

I will instruct you and teach you in the way you should go.

Psalm 32:8, NKJV

"When the Spirit of truth comes, he will guide you into all the truth, for he will not speak on his own authority, but whatever he hears he will speak, and he will declare to you the things that are to come."

John 16:13, ESV

$\mathscr{T}$RUST

The LORD is good, a refuge in times of trouble. He cares for those who trust in him.

Nahum 1:7, NIV

Regardless of who you are or what your circumstances may be, there comes a time in your life when you need someone you can fully trust. But people are often fickle and not to be trusted. Sometimes those you approach for help are so engrossed in their own problems that they have no time to assist you.

The joy of Christianity is the fact that God is only a prayer away. Whatever your problem or need, whenever it may occur, the Lord is waiting for you to turn to Him. Submit your problems to Him. He is omniscient and omnipotent, therefore you can rest assured that His way will eventually be to your benefit. The absolute trustworthiness of the risen Christ is your guarantee that God's way is the best for you. Therefore, when you are in need, turn to Him and allow Christ to enfold you with His love and to protect and encourage you.

THE TRIUMPH

OF TRUST

"Blessed is the man who trusts in the LORD, whose trust is the LORD. He is like a tree planted by water, that sends out its roots by the stream, and does not fear when heat comes."

Jeremiah 17:7-8, ESV

Trust in him at all times, O people; pour out your hearts to him, for God is our refuge.

Psalm 62:8, NIV

Unto thee, O LORD, do I lift up my soul. O my God, I trust in thee: let me not be ashamed, let not mine enemies triumph over me.

Psalm 25:1-2, KJV

What time I am afraid, I will trust in thee. In God I have put my trust; I will not fear what flesh can do unto me.

Psalm 56:3-4, KJV

"Let not your heart be troubled; you believe in God, believe also in Me."

John 14:1, NKJV

Trust in the LORD with all your heart, and do not lean on your own understanding. In all your ways acknowledge him, and he will make straight your paths.

Proverbs 3:5-6, ESV

Some trust in chariots and some in horses, but we trust in the name of the LORD our God.

Psalm 20:7, NIV

Trust in the LORD and do good; dwell in the land and enjoy safe pasture. Delight yourself in the LORD and he will give you the desires of your heart. Commit your way to the LORD; trust in him and he will do this: He will make your righteousness shine like the dawn, the justice of your cause like the noonday sun.

Psalm 37:3-6, NIV

Behold, this is our God; we have waited for Him, and He will save us. This is the LORD; we have waited for Him; we will be glad and rejoice in His salvation.

Isaiah 25:9, NKJV

Those who know Your name will put their trust in You; for You, Lord, have not forsaken those who seek You.

Psalm 9:10, NKJV

Our soul waits for the Lord; He is our help and our shield. For our heart shall rejoice in Him, because we have trusted in His holy name.

Psalm 33:20-21, NKJV

For the Scripture says, "Everyone who believes in him will not be put to shame."

Romans 10:11, ESV

Those who trust in the Lord are like Mount Zion, which cannot be shaken but endures forever.

Psalm 125:1, NIV

I am not ashamed, for I know whom I have believed, and I am convinced that he is able to guard until that Day what has been entrusted to me.

2 Timothy 1:12, ESV

$\mathcal{W}$EAKNESS

*My flesh and my heart may fail, but God is the
strength of my heart and my portion forever.*
Psalm 73:26, ESV

Perhaps you admire others for the mighty
works they do, and deep down in your
heart you desire to do the same. Perhaps
you made an effort in the past but failed
so miserably that you determined never to
try again. You accepted weakness as a flaw
in your character and decided that you can
do nothing to change it.

The only shameful thing about weakness
is to stop trying to overcome it. You were
born helpless, but you were not meant to
stay that way. You have the opportunity
to develop power and strength through
the grace of the almighty God. His power
will strengthen you to become the person
He meant you to be. Every weakness can
be overcome when you become aware that
God's own Spirit works in your spirit. You
will discover God-given talents and power
that give strength, purpose and inspiration
to your life.

THE WORD'S HELP

FOR THE WEAK

God is our refuge and strength, a very present help in trouble.

Psalm 46:1, KJV

The LORD God is my strength; He will make my feet like deer's feet, and He will make me walk on my high hills.

Habakkuk 3:19, NKJV

The eyes of the LORD run to and fro throughout the whole earth, to show Himself strong on behalf of those whose heart is loyal to Him.

2 Chronicles 16:9, NKJV

Fear thou not; for I am with thee: be not dismayed; for I am thy God: I will strengthen thee; yea, I will help thee; yea, I will uphold thee with the right hand of my righteousness.

Isaiah 41:10, KJV

He said to me, "My grace is sufficient for you, for My strength is made perfect in weakness." Therefore most gladly I will rather boast in my infirmities, that the power of Christ may rest upon me. Therefore I take pleasure in infirmities, in reproaches, in needs, in persecutions, in distresses, for Christ's sake. For when I am weak, then I am strong.

2 Corinthians 12:9-10, NKJV

The Lord is faithful, and he will strengthen and protect you from the evil one.

2 Thessalonians 3:3, NIV

I can do all things through Christ which strengtheneth me.

Philippians 4:13, KJV

The LORD is my rock and my fortress and my deliverer, my God, my rock, in whom I take refuge, my shield, and the horn of my salvation, my stronghold.

Psalm 18:2, ESV

O LORD, be gracious to us; we long for you. Be our strength every morning, our salvation in time of distress.

Isaiah 33:2, NIV

Those who trust in the LORD are like Mount Zion, which cannot be shaken but endures forever. As the mountains surround Jerusalem, so the LORD surrounds his people both now and forevermore.

Psalm 125:1-2, NIV

But I will sing of your strength; I will sing aloud of your steadfast love in the morning. For you have been to me a fortress and a refuge in the day of my distress. O my Strength, I will sing praises to you, for you, O God, are my fortress, the God who shows me steadfast love.

Psalm 59:16-17, ESV

May our Lord Jesus Christ himself and God our Father, who loved us and by his grace gave us eternal encouragement and good hope, encourage your hearts and strengthen you in every good deed and word.

2 Thessalonians 2:16-17, NIV

Likewise the Spirit helps us in our weakness. For we do not know what to pray for as we ought, but the Spirit himself intercedes for us with groanings too deep for words.

Romans 8:26, ESV

$\mathcal{S}$OURCES

The devotions included in this book have been drawn from the following sources:

1. De Villiers, Izak. 2002. *10 Ways to Overcome Disappointment.* Vereeniging: Christian Art Publishers.
2. Harvey, Edwin and Lillian 2002. *Kneeling We Triumph.* Vereeniging: Christian Art Publishers.
3. Mitchell, Fred. 1968. *At Break of Day.* Marshall: Morgan and Scott.
4. Ozrovech, Solly. 2002. *Fountains of Blessing.* Vereeniging: Christian Art Publishers.
5. Ozrovech, Solly. 2000. *The Glory of God's Grace.* Vereeniging: Christian Art Publishers.
6. Ozrovech, Solly. 2000. *Intimate Moments with God.* Vereeniging: Christian Art Publishers.
7. Ozrovech, Solly. 2000. *New Beginnings.* Vereeniging: Christian Art Publishers.
8. Ozrovech, Solly. 2002. *The Voice Behind You.* Vereeniging: Christian Art Publishers.
9. Tileston, Mary (compiler). 1951. *Daily Strength for Daily Needs.* London: Methuen.

OTHER BOOKS

IN THIS RANGE

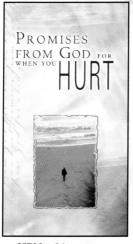

ISBN: 1-86920-071-3

ISBN: 1-86920-069-1

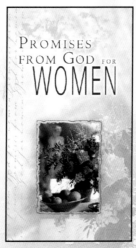

ISBN: 1-86920-070-5